It
ain't
over
till
it's
over

It ain't over till it's over

A user's guide to the second half of life

William E. Diehl and
Judith Ruhe Diehl

Augsburg Books
MINNEAPOLIS

Large-quantity purchases or custom editions of this book are available at a discount from the publisher. For more information, contact the sales department at Augsburg Fortress, Publishers, 1-800-328-4648, or write to: Sales Director, Augsburg Fortress, Publishers, P.O. Box 1209, Minneapolis, MN 55440-1209.

Scripture quotations are from the New Revised Standard Version of the Bible, copyright © 1989 by the Division of Christian Education of the National Council of the Churches of Christ in the USA. Used by permission.

Library of Congress Cataloging-in-Publication Data
Diehl, William E.
    It ain't over till it's over : a user's guide to the second half of life / William E. Diehl, Judith Ruhe Diehl.
    p. cm.
Includes bibliographical references.
    ISBN 0-8066-4448-6 (pbk. : alk. paper)
    1. Retirees—Religious life. 2. Retirement—Religious aspects—Christianity.
I. Diehl, Judith Ruhe. II. Title.
BV4596.R47 D54 2003
248.8'5—dc21   2002152640

Cover design by Ann Rezny
Book design by Michelle L. N. Cook
Cover art from Getty Images

The paper used in this publication meets the minimum requirements of American National Standard for Information Sciences—Permanence of Paper for Printed Library Materials, ANSI Z329.48-1984. ⊚ ™

Manufactured in the U.S.A.

07   06   05   04   03   1   2   3   4   5   6   7   8   9   10

contents

---

preface

The word *retire* evokes all sorts of images and emotions in the minds of different people. "Retire? You bet!" says a marketing manager in his sixties. "In three years we'll be off to Sun City, Arizona, where we can play golf every day and not have a care in the world."

"Retire? Are you kidding?" asks a self-employed computer specialist. "I'm only forty-six years old and haven't given it a thought."

"Retire? To what?" asks a hardworking restaurant owner. "We'll just end up in one of those nursing homes and spend the rest of our lives in utter boredom."

"Retire? We can hardly wait!" says a couple in their sixties. "We plan to move to Ohio where we can be near our grand-children and see them every day."

"Retire? I don't want to think about it," says a sixty-two-year-old university professor. "I like my work and don't ever want to leave it."

"Retire? That's a laugh! There is no such thing for women," says a woman who is a homemaker. "I will still do all the house-work wherever we go."

"Retire? One more year and we're out of here!" says a seventy-two-year-old auto salesman. "You can find us at Fort Lauderdale. We'll be on the beach every day."

"Retire? I never think about it," says a single mom of three. "All of my money goes to take care of my family, and my employer doesn't have a pension plan. I'll work until I drop."

"Retire? I hope so," says a baby boomer in her forties. "I doubt if Social Security will still be around twenty years from now."

"Retire? We are already retired," says two former teachers in their seventies. "But we have been so hurt by the big drop in the stock market that one of us may have to find work again."

The word *retire* means "to withdraw or go away or apart to a place of abode or shelter or seclusion." Some people look forward to retirement; for others, the word evokes fear and denial.

This book began in response to the urgings of a number of friends who said that no books have been written about Christian ministry in the senior years of life. There are books and articles about ministry *to* seniors in retirement, but nothing about ministry *by* seniors. In chapter 1, I make the case that the senior years are prime for contributing to the lives of others.

As I delved into the subject, it became more and more apparent that the book's audience should include persons well prior to the time of retirement, notably the so-called baby boomers. Rueful stories from persons recently retired from their jobs were convincing evidence that retirement living must begin with planning well before the event. This book is primarily directed to those fifty and above, but it wouldn't hurt for a forty-five-year-old to take a peek.

A major factor facing our society today is the increasing loss of "social capital"; that is, the organizations and institutions that hold things together in America. Robert Putnam, in his best-selling book *Bowling Alone*, convincingly points out how service clubs, fraternal organizations, neighborhoods, and school-, political-, and church-related organizations are receiving less volunteer support as elder members die and are not being replaced by the younger generations. Can more seniors be recruited for volunteer service and will the baby boomers spurn excessive individualism to take up the cause as they enter their retirement years? This is a major question the book considers, particularly in chapter 2.

A successful move into senior living requires some degree of planning, and planning begins with asking questions. What kind of lifestyle do I want? How many material possessions do I really need? Might I outlive my current assets? How can I show my gratitude to God for all my blessings? These are important questions. We will look at all of them, beginning in chapter 3.

In chapters 4 and 5, we will examine the important questions of living arrangements and lifestyle. I suggest key points seniors must consider.

The senior years can be characterized by freedom, growth, happiness, a deepening spirituality, and productive living. For some persons, especially those baby boomers who indulged themselves throughout the soaring 1990s, there will come a rude realization that work, not retirement, will consume most of their senior years. This is the topic of chapter 6.

For those who do not have to work in their senior years, there are seemingly boundless opportunities for Christian ministry through public service jobs, volunteering, and financial giving. But there must be a reality check of financial assets as we put our plans for senior living to work. Although we all knew that the soaring nineties had to come to an end sometime, the harsh reality of a recession in 2001 has sent many of us back to the drawing boards to reassess how much we can volunteer and give. We will consider these topics in chapters 7 and 8.

Financial topics will be discussed in this book, particularly in chapter 9. However, we will not get into much technical detail in the financial area. But we will ask the important questions, the answers for which can be found in hundreds of books and articles, and with advisors who deal with this topic specifically.

The extent to which the terrorist attacks of September 11, 2001, might affect life for seniors in the years ahead is difficult to predict. We will try to assess the effect of a war on terrorism.

Finally, in chapter 10, we will talk about one's view of death, how to help others with grief, and what we can do to make our own death easier on our family and loved ones.

I (William) am the primary author, assisted by my wife Judith, who will give her perspective at various points. I took early retirement from a senior management position in a Fortune 100 corporation at age fifty-six in order to form my own management-consulting corporation. Judith semi-retired from full-time child raising at age forty-six, to begin a second career as a politician, ultimately becoming the first woman ever elected to our Lehigh County Board of Commissioners. We both became the primary caregivers for our aging mothers.

Twice we voluntarily downsized our style of living as we moved into our senior years. We are now in our mid-seventies and live in a continuous care community. We have many stories to share about our own personal experiences to illustrate the topics being considered. Not everything has gone smoothly as we have moved through senior life, but we *have* walked our talk.

Much will be said in this book about the need for seniors to lead an active second half of life—to volunteer, to give, and to participate in community. But this is a book about spirituality *and* retirement, so I need to state my rock-bottom belief, at the outset, that I do not believe God's acceptance of me is based on my good works. Over and over Jesus emphasized the importance of faith; he said many times, "Your faith has made you whole."

It is because of the wonderful grace of God that Christians respond with good works. The good works represented in this book were not done in order to receive God's grace, but rather in thankfulness for the amazing grace of God, which we have already received through faith.

Judith and I are great advocates of ministry in daily life for all Christians. I have written seven previous books on the topic; Judith has written one. This book will argue that Christian ministry never stops. It is as essential in the years after retirement as it is in the earlier years. Ministry in daily life may change in style but it goes on, and as Yogi Berra said, "It ain't over till it's over."

William E. Diehl
Judith Ruhe Diehl
January 2003

chapter
one
retiring
retirement

Many people, when they think about retirement, imagine leaving their current work-a-day lives to a life of play and leisure. But is having such a life in our senior years really living? Is it healthy? Is it Christian? In this chapter, we explore a couple of understandings of "retirement"—and the effects such approaches have on seniors.

My grandfather Diehl, born in 1874, spent his entire working life as an employee of the U. S. Postal Service. He began as a young mail sorter and worked his way up a succession of jobs until he was appointed the postmaster of Allentown, Pennsylvania. He was always a healthy man: he prided himself on never missing a day of work due to illness, blizzards, or anything. He was up at 6:00 every morning, ate the hearty breakfast my grandmother prepared, and walked the mile down Hamilton Street to the post office. My grandmother, Nana, always packed a lunch for him, even when he became postmaster. Each evening he walked the mile home, had an ample supper, read the newspaper, and listened to his favorite radio programs. By 9:00 P.M. he was in bed.

On Sundays he and Nana regularly walked the one block to Christ Lutheran Church, and they always sat in the same pew. They had one child, my father, but he ran out on us when I was very young and was living with another woman. But my mother and I were also members of Christ Lutheran, and we frequently sat with Nana and Grandpa Diehl. Nana and Grandpa often invited us to dinner after the church service. Even as a youngster, I was surprised at the way Grandpa Diehl invariably criticized the pastor and his sermons.

On Sunday afternoons he and Nana sometimes took the trolley car—he never owned a car—to visit members of Nana's family.

Virtually all of Grandpa Diehl's life was consumed in his work and he loved it. I never heard him talk about retirement.

On the day he turned seventy, a district postal superintendent came and, in the presence of all the postal workers, gave Grandpa the traditional watch. He walked home that evening as usual, and left his career of forty-eight years behind him.

In his retirement he did nothing but read the newspaper, listen to the radio, eat, and sleep. He ventured out of the house only to go to church. Two years later he was dead.

As a young child, I was astonished that my robust grandfather, who had never missed a day of work, died so suddenly. Today, though, I understand. His whole life and identity were vested in his job. He had no other interests to fall back on. When his job ended, so did his identity, purpose, and reason to live. His body knew that and it just plain shut down.

Retirement killed my grandfather. He was a victim of "death by retirement."

My grandfather Yellis was also a loyal, hardworking man. He was the superintendent of a planing mill in a town about ten miles away. The company specialized in interior woodwork and cabinets for private homes, churches, and public buildings. He also never missed a day of work, sometimes driving through blizzards to get there.

He was well into his seventies when the owner of the mill died and his family closed the business. Retirement was thrust upon Grandpa Yellis unexpectedly.

Because of his many years of experience in woodwork, he turned their basement into a small shop. He had no power tools; he did everything by hand. Over the course of time he made three beautiful cherry blanket chests for each of his daughters, some elegant chancel chairs for his church, and assorted pieces of furniture for others.

He and Nana Yellis were faithful members of St. Michael's Lutheran Church in Allentown. Unlike Grandpa Diehl, he served on many committees and seemed to enjoy being a part of the congregation.

He also loved to draw. Primarily, he did colored-pencil drawings, from memory, of his homestead, including the planing mill, the millrace, and the river. They were somewhat in the style of Grandma Moses.

A few years after his retirement, Grandma Yellis had a stroke. Grandpa and their oldest unmarried daughter, Aunt Elsie, became her caregivers. Because my aunt worked, it fell to him to make the meals and to do most of the caring for his sick wife. But he still drove his car and got out to visit us until he was ninety.

When my grandmother died at age eighty-nine, he took to his drawing in earnest. Many of his colored-pencil drawings were done on the cardboard that came with his shirts from the laundry. He won several blue ribbons for his sketches at the Allentown Fair and was featured in our local newspaper. My aunt had two of his drawings converted into notepaper, which I still use occasionally.

He died at age ninety-five, four years after my grandmother's death. After his death, we came across scores of his drawings. They now hang on our walls and on the walls of his two other grandchildren and several great-grandchildren.

Grandpa Yellis avoided "death by retirement" because he always felt his life had a purpose: caring for his sick wife, making lovely furniture for his family and his church, and turning out colored-pencil sketches of his homestead to give to others.

I have interviewed scores of people in preparing to write this book. I have talked with men and women who have been in retirement for many years; I have talked with men and women who are recently retired or going through the process of retirement; and I have talked with many baby boomers. Some are thinking about retirement; some are not. Some smile and say, "I have already retired from four jobs and will probably retire from a few more."

Everyone talks about retirement in the language of "what I am doing" (or will be doing), but it has been interesting to observe that the "doing" breaks down into an inward focus or an outward expression. Sometimes it can be both. As people enter the years of retirement, they may do things for their own pleasure or they may do things for the pleasure of others. Those who do things for their own pleasure have difficulty articulating a meaning or purpose in their lives. Those who do things for others always can talk about meaning or purpose in their lives.

The last boss I had before I became a national manager of sales was an active and energetic sales manager. Lynn was extremely well versed in his field and highly respected nationally. He was devoted to his job, but he did have one other passion— golf. The sales-manager position naturally fit in with customer golf. He and his wife, Bernice, lived next door to their golf club. He played with friends regularly on Saturdays and in a Wednesday evening golf league.

Lynn did not look forward at all to his mandatory retirement age of sixty-five. He dreaded it and didn't mind telling people so. But he always concluded his comments on retirement by saying, "Well, at least I'll be able to give my full time to golf."

Very soon after his retirement, Lynn and Bernice sold their home and moved into an elegant condominium on the Atlantic Coast of Florida. The condominium development had its own golf course. In phone calls to him, he always sounded cheery and seemed to be enjoying his life. He had met three other recent retirees and they formed a "steady foursome," as he described it.

His day was like this: Up at 7:00 A.M. Read the morning newspaper. Breakfast with Bernice. Meet the other three golf buddies at the club around 10:00. Play the front nine. Eat lunch together. Play the back nine. Play four-handed gin rummy in the clubhouse for about an hour. Return to his apartment to shower and shave and get dressed for dinner. Have cocktails with "steady foursome," including their wives, at one of the other three's apartment and then on to dinner at the club. Back to his apartment after dinner to watch some television and then on to bed.

Every day was exactly like that, day after day. He tried to keep in touch with old business acquaintances but, as time passed, he was more and more out of the loop, with nothing left but golf.

"Don't you get tired of the same routine every day?" I once asked him in a phone conversation.

"Why should I?" he snapped back. "I love golf and I'm in a nice condo in Florida. I have three good friends, and Bernice and I are healthy. What more could I ask?"

I thought about it. Gone were the many business friends he enjoyed so much. Gone were the business goals and problems that called upon his keen mind. Gone were the people in his sales department who respected his vast experience and depended upon him for mentoring.

Lynn was lively and fairly active in his retirement. Problems with walking caused him to give up golf in his later years. He lived to be eighty-nine. But the active and creative leadership skills that characterized the man I worked for died long before his body did. There no longer was a real purpose in his life. He had experienced a form of "death in retirement." My friend Will Boyer frequently says, "I don't want to die before I die." His active life in many fields supports his philosophy.

Marc Freedman, president of Civic Ventures, an organization dedicated to expanding the social contributions to society of older Americans, quotes a retired doctor who was volunteering at

Samaritan Medical Clinic in San Mateo, California, as saying he did it because "I just didn't want to be unnecessary."[1]

In my book, talented people who do nothing but indulge themselves have made themselves "unnecessary." Playing a round or two of golf every week helps maintain one's health. For these reasons it is okay. But playing golf or tennis, or sailing, or fishing every day makes such activities the centerpiece of one's life, and they become one's god.

Women and Retirement

Many women, particularly in the generations preceding the baby boomers, spent their adult lives caring for families rather than being engaged in paid employment. This has financial ramifications in that such women get no social security and do not have pensions in their own names. For many of them, too, the act of retirement never happens. They move from one stage of adulthood into another—from marriage and homemaking to children and homemaking to middle and old age and homemaking. Reaching the state of retirement at an appropriate age, a woman merely continues with her interests, perhaps with more uncommitted time at her discretion.

Much is changing in this regard. We have three daughters and they, along with 55 percent of their cohorts, *do* work outside the home. For them, there might eventually be three retirements: from raising a child, from a paid job, and from major homemaking.

It is a sad reality that some women feel they must list themselves as retired when their husband retires from his job. This can be especially true for women who have not had a career outside the home, or whose careers have been "secondary" to their husband's. "My husband just retired and now he thinks I'm retired, too," laments one active senior friend. "He expects me to do what he wants to do."

Defining Retirement

As noted earlier, the dictionary definition of the verb *retire* can be summed up as "to go away, depart for a rest, seclusion, or shelter. To withdraw from business or public life as to live in leisure on one's income, savings, or pension."

The adjective *retired* is generally defined as "withdrawn, secluded, withdrawn from business or public life."

The definition of the noun *retirement* is generally stated as: (1) the act of retiring, (2) the state of being retired, and (3) the state of withdrawal from one's position or occupation or from active working life.

The word *retire* appears in the Bible only twice, as does the word *retirement*. But in all four instances, the reference is to armies or people "retiring from battle."

There are a number of times in the New Testament when Jesus withdrew from the crowds to be in a quiet place where he could pray. There is not the least suggestion that Jesus wanted to withdraw from his work itself. But rather it was for a specific time of prayer. The closest reference to one leaving one's occupation "to live in leisure on one's income, savings, or pension" is the scathing parable Jesus told about the rich landowner:

> The land of a rich man produced abundantly. And he thought to himself, "What should I do, for I have no place to store my crops?" Then he said, "I will do this: I will pull down my barns and build larger ones, and there I will store all my grain and my goods. And I will say to my soul, 'Soul, you have ample goods laid up for many years; relax, eat, drink, be merry.'" But God said to him, "You fool! This very night your life is being demanded of you. And the things you have prepared, whose will they be?" So it is with those who store up treasures for themselves but are not rich toward God. (Luke 12:16-21)

There is no suggestion in the Bible that people retired from their work. Nor does that notion appear in any early human history.

In fact, retirement, as we now define it, has not been possible for the vast masses of people throughout history. It was a possibility only among the very wealthy. Even today, retirement is not a possibility among most of the world's population. That includes many low-income people in the United States. You work until you drop or are cared for by your children or become dependent upon welfare programs.

So where did the notion of retirement come from?

Etymologists indicate that the word *retirement*, meaning the withdrawal from an occupation or business activity, is first attested to in 1648 in Oliver Cromwell's *Letters*, quoted by Carlyle.[2]

In 1799, George Washington said, "Retirement is as necessary to me as it will be welcome."[3]

The earliest most specific use of our contemporary definition of retirement appeared in the March 12, 1885, *Manchester Examiner*, which stated "The retirement of Mr. Beith from the chairmanship of the Executive is a just cause for regret."[4]

It appears that our present definition of retirement as "withdrawal from one's position or occupation or from active working life" is an outgrowth of the Industrial Revolution. It does not have a long history.

Note that the dictionary definitions of *retirement* refer both to the act of retiring from one's business or profession and to the state of being retired. Most people use the word in both senses, but I argue that in today's culture, and for Christians in particular, retirement is an event but cannot be a state of life. There are very few people today who, like my Grandpa Diehl, retire from decades of work with the same organization to withdraw from life. As stated earlier, some baby boomers claim to have "retired" six or eight times, meaning they left one job for another. Such a retirement was an event, not a state of life.

The first question people commonly ask of each other at parties and other gatherings is "What do you do?" If I say I am an accountant, or doctor, or homemaker, or architect, the question is answered. But if I say "I am retired," another question or two invariably follows. "What are you doing now?" is perhaps the most common. Or the question "Retired from what?" is posed. In any event, saying "I am retired" does not describe what I am doing now. It merely informs the other person that at some time in my past, I left the work that was my primary occupation for some or most of my life.

We have a church directory in which we list the names, addresses, phone numbers, and current occupations of all our members. We want our people to know where their fellow members live out their ministries in daily life. The listings also provide us with the ability to gather together persons in similar occupations for educational programs or services of affirmation.

As I go down the list in our church directory, the occupations read like this: chemist, scientist, homemaker, retired, attorney, retired, contractor, self-employed, dental hygienist, retired. Now I happen to know what most of those retired people are doing. One of them is a volunteer manager of our local Meals-on-Wheels. Another is a part-time computer consultant for the company from which he officially retired. Another is a volunteer literacy tutor for high school kids. One travels all over the world as a consultant for the Evangelical Lutheran Church in America. His wife is the president of the local League of Women Voters. I frequently hear them say, "I am busier now than when I was working."

My efforts to have people list their postretirement occupations in our church directory usually go nowhere. In our society you are either in a full-time job or you are retired. Yet there are scores of people in our congregation who are spending many hours in part-time work, volunteering, or consulting. They are carrying out ministries in and to the world. They have not withdrawn from public life.

We fail to recognize the fact that more people are living longer and are using their senior years in activities that were not possible for most people fifty years ago. Furthermore, more people are retiring from their full-time work at earlier ages. In 1965, 57 percent of people over age fifty-five were in the workforce. By 1995, that number had dropped to 38 percent. According to a survey by the Center for Workforce Development at Rutgers University, 76 percent of the baby boomer generation wants to retire before age sixty, and 81 percent of generation X wants to do the same.[5]

There is voluminous research on the condition of older Americans, and just about all of it shows that most retirees today are healthier than any previous generation of older people. They are also wealthier and say they feel happier than most Americans of all ages. They make up 30 percent of all cruise passengers and 20 percent of all first-time passport recipients. The poverty roll is lower for the elderly than for people under the age of sixty-five: 10.5 percent today compared with 13.6 percent in 1947.[6]

Of course, there are some people whose retirement does fit the definition of "withdrawn from one's position or occupation or from an active working life." My former boss who retired from an active working life to move to Florida and spend every day playing golf is an example. Same for my Grandpa Diehl, who sat in the same chair every day, reading the newspaper and listening to radio.

What a waste of human capital when healthy, active, creative, responsible people retire to a life of self-indulgence such as golf or sailing or fishing every day. What a waste of human resources when people retire to build huge homes or buy elegant vacation condos. In a time when they could be giving something back to society, they squander all their time and financial resources on themselves. From the perspective of a Christian, such total self-indulgence is more than a waste of one's life; it is directly contrary to what Jesus taught about love of self and neighbor.

"Senior Living" not "Retirement"

If we confine the word *retirement* to the act of leaving one's primary occupation, what word should we use to replace retirement as a stage in life?

In Britain there is a movement to speak of three stages of life. The first stage (from birth to age twenty-five) is the preparatory stage. The second stage (twenty-five to fifty-five) are the working years. The third stage (fifty-five to eighty-five) is the giving-back stage.[7] This is an interesting proposal, but the notion of stages would require an entirely new vocabulary for lifetime passages.

Why don't we simply adopt the word that is already commonly used in America: senior? We already refer to senior citizens. Let's shorten it to seniors. We now have a senior Professional Golfers' Association, a senior discount for movies, public transportation, restaurants, and retail stores. Why don't we simply refer to anyone over age fifty-five as a senior? Most senior discounts and other privileges define fifty-five as the minimum age for recipients. Fifty-five is the minimum age for the residents of the Luther Crest Retirement Community, where Judith and I now live. (I think it would be much more realistic to call it the Luther Crest *Senior* Community.)

Here and there one finds hints that age fifty may soon become the entry point for our culture's recognition of seniors. The American Association of Retired People (AARP), for example, begins soliciting members at the age of fifty.

As the baby boomers begin to retire, it seems silly to refer to them as baby boomer retirees; baby boomer seniors might make more sense.

Why make such a big fuss over words? Here's why: Many people—perhaps too many—approach the years of retirement with the notion that it is the stage of withdrawal from active life to a life of self-indulgence.

Total self-indulgence, at any age, is unchristian. God has given many of us the gift of longer years of life than previous generations. We can use these years in savoring the gifts of God's creation in music, literature, travel, friendships, and in remaining active in serving other people who are less fortunate.

Throughout the rest of this book I will use the word *retirement* solely as an event in one's life, and I will use the word *senior* for the post-fifty-five stage of life. The book is, however, also written for the benefit of those approaching senior status.

I have retired the words *retirement* and *retire* as a stage of life. It no longer makes sense in today's culture.

chapter
two
being
necessary

On Thursday morning the phone rings. It is the volunteer coordinator for our county Meals-on-Wheels. Could Judith and I possibly fill in on a route for Friday morning? We check our calendars and yes, we can. We had done our regular route two days earlier, but we are needed again.

The calls for substitutes for Meals-on-Wheels have become more frequent. Most of the "steadies" are well over sixty-five and, as they age and require additional medical attention, there are more occasions when substitutes are needed. As yet, very few baby boomers are substituting, much less becoming regular drivers. Yet the number of people out there depending upon us for meals continues to grow.

A senior physician who volunteers at a clinic for poor people says he chose to volunteer because "I just didn't want to be unnecessary." Well, there are so many areas of our society where the involvement of seniors is necessary that those of us who claim to be followers of Jesus Christ have no excuse to not give of ourselves.

In the presidential election of 2000, I decided to do some campaigning for my candidate. I was shocked to discover that there no longer was a political party organization in my county. "Can't get people to come out and work" was the reason given by one of the long-time party activists. I even had a hard time finding a bumper sticker for my car.

There were absolutely no presidential political buttons in our county. Some for local election contests, yes, but not for national. "It's all dependent upon television," my friend continued. "Send your money to the national campaign office," he urged.

My mind flew back to the first year I ever worked in a presidential election. It was for Dwight Eisenhower. The campaign had a city office and precinct offices in Detroit. They sent me brochures and pins and gave me a map of the houses I was to visit. Each weekend I walked through neighborhoods; even though we all had television in those days, campaigns still depended upon volunteers going door-to-door. Precinct leaders closely tabulated both the voter turnout and the votes cast for the party candidates. That was the measure by which we were judged as workers. Allowance was made, of course, for party registration, but if your district had a better turnout of registered voters in your party and if the vote was higher than usual for your party, you were on the list for more campaign work in the future. All the tasks, from neighborhood campaigner to county party leader, were handled by volunteers. Today I have to search hard to find a bumper sticker and there are simply no buttons or leaflets to hand out.

For years, Judith has been a member of the local League of Women Voters. I always go with her to their annual legislative dinner meeting. Over the years I have seen the attendance decrease as older members die or are incapacitated. Fewer younger women are joining.

I was asked to speak at a local Rotary Club recently. The person who invited me warned that attendance would be low, and it was: only eight attended. "We used to have average attendances of forty," the program leader explained. "Now our membership is less than twenty."

When Judith and I were youngsters, the Women's Club was a major influence in our city. They had their own building, which was used for various civic events. In the past twenty years, membership has dropped dramatically. They recently disbanded and sold their building to the local bar association.

The Elks Club used to have a building with a ballroom where many dances were held during World War II. Today there is no longer an Elks Club.

These experiences of decreased volunteers for Meals-on-Wheels, political campaigns, and clubs are simply illustrations of a national trend that Robert D. Putnam calls "civic disengagement." Putnam reports that this has been going on for the past twenty years. In his best-selling book *Bowling Alone: The Collapse and Revival of American Community*,[1] Putnam gives overwhelming evidence that Americans have been drifting away from every form of voluntary association.

Bowling Alone received high praise throughout the national press.[2] In the *Christian Century*, Mark Chaves summarized the book as follows:

> With stunning consistency, virtually every indicator of civic engagement currently available shows the same pattern of increase followed by stagnation and decline—newspaper reading; TV news watching; attending public meetings; petition signing; running for public office; serving as an officer or committee member in any local clubs or organizations; writing letters to the editor; participating in local meetings of national organizations; attending religious services; . . . playing sports; . . . donating money as a percentage of income; working on community projects; giving blood.[3]

In the first two-thirds of Putnam's book, he describes in great detail the social dislocation of Americans in the past twenty years. He claims that the cause of this dislocation is not so much the withdrawal of volunteers from active involvement as it is the dying off of older volunteers without the replacement of younger ones. He then devotes a section to the importance of building up social capital; that is, the network that connects Americans to each other. Finally, Putnam suggests an "Agenda for Social Capitalists." This part of the book, most reviewers have agreed, is the weakest. He sets out challenges but does not suggest how they can be met and, most importantly, who will do it.

And here we come to the primary point of *It Ain't Over Till It's Over*. It must be the agenda of all those in or entering the years of senior living to reverse the behavioral trends that lead to social dislocation. Christians need to lead the way. It is more than simply our agenda; it is our calling as Christians.

Who will fill the dwindling ranks of civic volunteers? How about the next generation—can we count on the baby boomers?

Baby Boomers in Context

There is a growing controversy about the future of retirement for baby boomers. This group, born between 1946 and 1964, represents a large population increase. When age distribution bar charts are drawn, the baby boom has been likened to a photo of a large animal passing through the body of a snake. The bulge is significantly larger than the previous generation or the succeeding generation.

For the purposes of this book, we will use the shorthand "DWW2" generation for those born between 1920 and 1945, meaning they were children of the Great Depression and World War II. The baby boom generation is roughly from 1946 to 1964. Children born between 1965 and 1983 are generation X, and those born between 1984 and 2005 we will refer to as generation Y. The forecast for the year 2020 is that there will be a total population of 322,742,000 Americans, of which 73,099,000 (23 percent) will be baby boomers.

The leading edge of the baby boom is fast approaching the age of retirement and some early birds have already retired. The influx of boomers reaching retirement age is being hailed by many social scientists as a golden age for volunteerism in this country.

The most optimistic champion of the baby boom is Marc Freedman, author of *Prime Time: How Baby Boomers Will Revolutionize Retirement and Transform America.*[4] Freedman is president of Civic Ventures, a nonprofit organization based in San Francisco that works to expand the social contribution of older Americans to society, and to help transform the aging American society into a source of individual and social revival.

Another champion of the potential of retiring baby boomers is Dr. Jack McConnell of Hilton Head, South Carolina. Looking ahead to the next two decades when millions of baby boomers will be retiring, Dr. McConnell hopes that many of the doctors, nurses, and other health professionals among them will mobilize to volunteer in clinics that provide free health care to people without health insurance.

In 1998, Dr. McConnell founded Volunteers in Medicine to see if his idea would work. Last year retired people who volunteered their time provided $4 million of care to some 13,000 patients. The clinic is being hailed by experts as the kind of cutting-edge volunteer program that will attract a new generation of baby boomers.[5]

A survey conducted by Peter D. Hart Research Associates suggests that currently, retired persons consider volunteering in a positive light. Half of over 800 Americans polled from ages fifty to seventy-five said that they consider helping nonprofit organizations to be "fairly important" or "very important" in their retirement years. The report predicted that over the next few decades charities could see an increase in the number of senior people who want to volunteer. The survey also found that Americans who have not yet retired place a higher priority on volunteering than do those who have already retired.[6] Sounds very promising, doesn't it? But wait a minute. Not everyone agrees.

Demographers see something else. "The vast majority of boomers delayed work, delayed marriage, delayed childbirth, and delayed growing up," says Peter Francese, former president of *American Demographics* magazine. "They're now spending a fortune on delaying the onset of old age. They've always done everything later, and you can bet they'll delay retirement."[7]

Many boomers will continue to work simply because they enjoy it. But many more will have a more important reason to remain gainfully employed: they cannot afford to retire.

As we talk about baby boomers, care must be taken not to generalize the character of *all* persons born between the years of 1946 and 1964. Nor can we assume that the entire World War II generation has been, is now, or will be active in volunteering. According to Peter D. Hart's research, 32 percent of seniors chose retirement as "a time to take it easy, take care of yourself, enjoy leisure activities and take a much-deserved rest from work and daily responsibilities."[8] In other words, one-third of *my* generation see their senior years as years of self-indulgence.

A study conducted for the American Association of Retired Persons by the Roper Storch organization found that only 16 percent of the 2,000 respondents in the baby boomer age brackets said they would not work in their retirement. Of the 80 percent who did plan to remain employed, about one-third said the main reason would be financial, while the other two-thirds said they would labor for the love of it.

A second study, conducted by the Employee Benefits Research Institute based in Washington, D.C., reports that 68 percent of the boomer respondents expect to draw a job-related paycheck in retirement. This is up from 61 percent in 1998.[9]

Moreover, many boomers are falsely confident about their ability to afford retirement. For years the investment community has been warning boomers of the need to save for retirement. Another report from the Employee Benefits Research Institute states that sums set aside by boomers for retirement are "generally unimpressive."[10]

In fact, many boomers, caught up in the euphoria of the soaring 1990s, are confident, almost arrogant, about their special status in life. "Boomers are a special, blessed generation," writes Brian O'Reilly. "The tedious rules that applied for our parents just don't apply for us. First of all, old age simply isn't going to happen. We're permanently young, almost by definition. Who ever heard of geezer-boomers?"

Mr. O'Reilly, the writer of that article, confessed that when his managing editor gave him the assignment to write about the boomers and retirement, he first felt it was a compliment. "Somewhere on the way back to my office it hit me," he writes. "I'm clueless about retirement, and he (the editor) knows it."[11]

Two factors, apart from their ignorance of retirement, will provide incentives for boomers to continue working for pay. First, the delayed-retirement credit, which is the reward for deferring receipt of social security benefits, is gradually rising.

Second, the generation X population is smaller in number. By 2020 there will be several million fewer people aged thirty-five to fifty-four than there are today, even though there will probably be many more jobs that need to be filled. Generation X will not be able to meet the labor demand. Employers will be motivated to provide incentives to keep older boomers working.

Those who anticipate a flood of baby boomer volunteers have also pointed out that people are retiring younger than they used to. That used to be true, but even that trend has reversed as baby boomers enter the senior years. According to Peter D. Hart Research Associates, in 1950, 81 percent of men sixty-two and older were in the work force. By 1985 this figure had dropped to 51 percent. But the trend has reversed and in 1990 it was up to 54 percent and climbing.[12]

So it is not at all certain that the baby boomers will provide vast numbers of retirees who will fill the badly needed vacancies in civic and social organizations. Moreover, the baby boomers have not had a great reputation for volunteering.

Edward Esse, volunteering specialist for AARP in Pennsylvania, has this to say about the likelihood of baby boomers doing volunteer work in retirement: "One thing of concern to AARP is that this generation is more inclined to participate in public need with money than volunteer service. Money does everything. They were raised with this attitude. The money is there; the service is not always there."[13]

None of our four children has invested their time in doing the kind of volunteering Judith and I have done all our lives. But there are such great differences in our family situations that it is difficult to make comparisons. For example, during my working years at Bethlehem Steel Company, I earned enough money to support our family without Judith having to work for pay. Our four children, much to our delight, have chosen careers in which they directly serve others. Our son and our youngest daughter are in education. Our middle daughter is a nurse with an advanced degree, working in a social service organization that helps dysfunctional families. Our oldest daughter is a lawyer who has given all her time to pro bono justice issues. All four are in fields that do not pay well, but they are committed to serving others. In short, they are already serving society in their worklives. I cannot claim to have done that in my work as a steel salesman.

Although the baby boomer is stereotypically pictured as working very long hours in high-tech or investment fields, the 46 percent of them who are married with children generally have two wage earners. Some boomers are still paying off college loans. Some live in large homes, with three-car garages, swimming pools, and many indoor amenities—the boom years of the 1990s gave them the courage to undertake large mortgages. In fact, some of them confided in me that they were one paycheck away from bankruptcy, and the recession of 2000–2002 did, unfortunately, cause some to declare themselves bankrupt.

My generation, DWW2, was fortunate. As we returned from World War II we received assistance from the federal government. We were able to get a virtually free college education. Government-insured, low-interest mortgages were the means for us to buy our first homes. Real estate inflation from the fifties through the nineties helped us to "buy up" every time we moved.

The September 11 terrorist attacks in New York and Washington, D.C., and our nation's subsequent declaration of war against all terrorists, wherever they may be, brought the citizens of our country together in a way not experienced since World War II. People of all ages united in an outpouring of money and volunteerism. "What can we do to help?" was heard from all parts of the country. How long this support will remain so strong is impossible to predict.

The economy, which was already sliding into recession in 2000, was further damaged by the terrorist activities. A steep drop in the stock market had a major effect on many pension funds and individual IRA accounts, including our own. Polls showed that the result of all of the above caused people to review their personal values. Consumer purchasing plunged (except for the automobile industry, which offered 0 percent financing on most of their cars). Early polls of American values showed that material goods were less important to people and that more people were turning to God. Only time will tell if this shift in values was permanent.

So the question remains: Will there be enough financially able, socially committed baby boomers to fully replace the diminishing army of volunteers and civic activists of my generation? The jury on that question will be out for a number of years; however, there are some signs for hope. On January 30, 2002, President George W. Bush, in his State of the Union address, called upon all Americans to commit at least two years or 4,000 hours over the rest of their lifetimes to the service of their neighbors and their nation. He specifically urged more volunteering for the Peace Corps, AmeriCorps, Senior Corps (see chapter 7: "Volunteering") and a newly created Freedom Corps. The extent to which the president can mobilize citizens to do more volunteering will determine whether we begin to build up social capital.

There is another positive sign. generation Y, those born after 1983, may well be more active in civic life than the boomers and generation X. The leading edge of Generation Y can now be found on college campuses. And the report on their social concerns, activism, and volunteering is encouraging. "Activism is indeed a reality all across American higher education," reports Arthur Levine in his article "A New Generation of Student Protesters Arises."[14]

Mr. Levine reported on a study he conducted with an independent scholar, Jeanette S. Cureton. They surveyed 9,100 undergraduates, including focus-group interviews with students on twenty-eight campuses. Also surveyed were 270 chief student affairs officers. They found that 64 percent of the 9,100 undergraduates were involved in volunteer work such as Habitat for Humanity or raising funds and collecting clothes for persons in need of housing in their communities. "That was true of students at two-year and four-year colleges, of students in every region of the country, of male and female, older and younger, residential and non-residential and full-time and part-time students," he writes.

The article goes on to report on student protests that tend to be issue oriented rather than the ideological student protests of the 1960s. Because protest actions are focused locally instead of nationally, the press has not caught up with what is happening. It is invisible to the public. There is one area of concern, however: the generation Y population has shown little interest in national politics, and those who are old enough to vote seldom do so.

Some of my friends at Muhlenberg College answer yes to my question as to whether their students are more active in volunteerism than students ten years ago. They add, however, that college administrations are encouraging this volunteerism much more in recent years, and that may be the students' motivation.

That is also true of our local high schools. Students are being encouraged to do volunteer work in the community. We have had some instances in which students were required to do volunteer community work as part of a social studies course. Some parents rebelled at such requirements of their children, but, generally, the local volunteering continues.

Another local mark of student interests in social needs is the large turnouts for walks that raise funds, through pledges, for charities and other causes, and for benefit performances. Participants are often well below high-school age. Will the community volunteering of high school and college days carry over into the years of full-time work?

What employers will do is a big factor. During periods of low unemployment, where employers are trying hard to secure and maintain employees, there has been a fair degree of released time for employees to work in community projects. Mike Kennelly, thirty-seven years old and a managing partner with a national accounting firm in Chicago, devotes about twelve hours a week to a mentoring and tutoring program he created in 1991. The program serves inner-city children ages five to fourteen. Since the program began, about 250 employees have become involved in the program; in 2000, the company's practice donated $14 million worth of time, with about 25 percent of 30,000 employees taking part in company-sponsored programs.

At Shared Vision, a fifty-person technology-consulting firm in New York City, employees get one fully paid week off a year to do volunteer work for any charity.[15]

The United Way, cognizant of the need for volunteers, has been encouraging employers to give some free time to those employees who want to work as volunteers. How well this will continue in periods of high unemployment is anyone's guess. Hopefully, the experience gained through company-sponsored volunteering will carry over into baby boomer retirement years.

My guess is this: My generation, DWW2, can keep volunteering alive until we are about eighty years old. Fueled by President George W. Bush's 2002 initiatives to develop greater service to the nation, an increasing number of baby boom and generation X people will come forward to fill in for the loss of DWW2 seniors. Generation Y people will then begin to join in and thus create a positive swing toward building more social capital.

Voting

There is something special about those who vote.

In *Bowling Alone*, Robert Putnam states that "voters are more likely to be interested in politics, to give to charity, to volunteer, to serve on juries, to attend community school board meetings, to participate in public demonstrations, and to cooperate with their fellow citizens on community affairs."[16]

America's record is not good. For the past thirty years there has been a steady decline in voter turnout for presidential elections. Turnout for presidential elections and local elections has declined approximately 25 percent in the past thirty-six years.[17] Fewer Americans vote than in all twenty-two other established democracies, except Switzerland, which has a slightly lower rate than the United States.[18]

Putnam states that "virtually all the long-run decline in turnout is due to the gradual replacement of voters who came of age before or during the New Deal and World War II by the generations who came of age later."[19] So why aren't the baby boomers voting? Back in 1985, there appeared a best-selling book, *Habits of the Heart: Individualism and Commitment in American Life*, by Robert Bellah, Richard Madsen, William Sullivan, Ann Swidler, and Stephen Tipton.[20] The authors argued convincingly that the age-old American tension between private interest and the public good had swung too much toward individualism at the expense of a commitment to public virtue.

And therein probably lies the distinction. Those of us who went through the Great Depression and World War II participated in two national crises. Personal sacrifice for the common good was expected by and for all. I clearly remember in the depression years how we shared and cared for each other as best we could. And I was a part of that huge national commitment to defeat common enemies, even with the knowledge that it might cost our lives.

But following World War II came a huge economic boom. Consumer goods, which were scarce during the war, began to flood our markets. The 1950s were years of recovering from the war and the following decade was called the Soaring Sixties. Aided by the medium of commercial television, the focus of self-interest gained more and more at the expense of public good.

John F. Kennedy, in his 1961 presidential inaugural address, probably sensed this swing, for he implored America to "Ask not what your country can do for you, ask what you can do for your country." This idealism gave way increasingly to the oft-repeated quote of later presidential candidates, "Are you better off now than you were four years ago?" And in 1992, candidate Bill Clinton constantly reminded his campaign committee, "It's the economy, stupid."

An interesting statistic relating to the tension between individualism and the common good comes out of the television ratings during the 2000 presidential campaign. There were 37.7 million viewers of the third Bush-Gore presidential debate while, at the same time, 51 million people watched the final episode of *Survivor*.[21] Poor as they may have been, the presidential debates dealt with issues of the common good. *Survivor* was a series that scorned any suggestion of common good but championed the one person who could outlast all others, at total expense of virtue. (It is interesting to compare the 37.7 million viewers of the final 2000 presidential debate with the 70 million viewers of the final Nixon-Kennedy debate in 1960.)

Baby boomers are not the only ones less concerned about politics; generation X, the generation following the boomers, is even less interested. Daily newspaper readerships among people under thirty-five dropped from two-thirds in 1965 to one-third in 1990, at the same time that television news viewing in this same age group fell from 52 percent to 41 percent.[22]

In defense of the baby boomers, they were born, raised, and indoctrinated with a culture that championed individualism and self-interest, while the depression and World War II generation sat back and let it happen. Why? Because we seniors benefited from the same economic gains that stole the hearts of our children and we did not know how to counter the culture of individualism.

Nevertheless, we seniors still are regular voters. Until the voting trend reverses itself, as hopefully it will with today's college and high school students, we seniors must continue to be informed and involved in our nation's political process as much as we are physically able. Once more, we are necessary.

In all three of the synoptic Gospels (Matthew, Mark, and Luke), the story appears of how the Pharisees and Herodians tried to trap Jesus by asking if it was lawful for them to pay taxes to the emperor. Jesus responded by asking them whose title and image appeared on a coin. They responded by saying the emperor's.

Then Jesus said, "Give therefore to the emperor the things that are the emperor's, and to God the things that are God's" (Matt. 22:21; see also Mark 12:17 and Luke 20:25). Notice that Jesus does not limit his answer to taxes only. He says "the things that are the emperor's." In our democracy we have no emperor, but we elect presidents, governors, legislators, mayors, and other officials. We understand that we must pay taxes to the jurisdictions they govern. But we also must vote in order to decide who will govern those jurisdictions.

Now here is a "just suppose" question. Just suppose that in those days the people elected their emperor, and just suppose the Pharisees asked Jesus if it was lawful for them to pay taxes and vote. Do you think Jesus would have included taxes as those due the emperor, but not votes? I think not. I think that as Christians, we must vote just as we must pay taxes.

My mother, who died on her ninety-ninth birthday, was always interested in local and national politics. While she was mobile she never missed voting. When she no longer could get out, she regularly got absentee ballots and sent them in. Even when she no longer could sign her name, she made her X in the signature box. Just so with us. How long do we seniors continue to vote? You got it: "It ain't over till it's over." Are we seniors necessary? You bet we are.

As Putnam points out in Bowling Alone, it is vital to the well-being of American society that excessive individualism give way to concern for community. We seniors, who were raised in a time when there had to be a commitment to community, are needed to lead a culture of individualism away from its self-indulgence toward a society that links us together in mutual concern.

As Christians who have been called into community at our baptism, we have a special ministry in and to our society.

chapter three

planning for senior living

When it comes to planning, there are two types of people: those who plan ahead and anticipate some degree of control over their lives, and those who are relaxed about the future and are content to be controlled by, or at least go with the flow of, external events.

Judith and I are almost the opposites in planning. I, with my degree in engineering and my past work experience in strategic planning, believe in careful planning. It is not an obsession, but sometimes my family feels it is. Judith is much more relaxed about planning. She does plan some things—she always planned, for example, to have a large family—but generally she waits for opportunities to come along.

But planning or not, it is our values that greatly influence what we do in the senior years of life. On values, Judith and I agree. We value having a good family and good friends. We value a faith that says we should give thanks to God for all our blessings and show our thanks through our ministry to others. We value simplicity in life. We do not value a life focused on material goods or self-indulgence. We value education, good music, good books, and good conversations.

In this chapter, we will examine how planning makes a difference for senior living.

What follows is the way each of us planned for and moved into our senior years.

Bill's Story

I first began thinking about changing careers after I turned fifty. I liked my job at Bethlehem Steel very much. I had a responsible position as national sales manager for construction steels and was earning a six-figure salary (back in 1976), plus excellent benefits. Since we had sales offices and fabricating shops all over the country, I was able to travel, which I like to do. I had a membership at the Saucon Valley County Club, which is well known for its three elegant golf courses. My top management was very supportive and pretty much let me run the business—as long as we showed a profit.

Because the company wanted to maintain an image of a good corporate citizen, I was encouraged to accept requests to serve on local civic and social agency boards. At various times I was president of the local United Way, on the boards of the United Way of Pennsylvania, the local legal service agency, the governor's committee on legal services, the Lehigh County Community Council, and other agencies. My health was good and my spiritual life was nourished in an active Lutheran church, and I served the church through membership on the Executive Council of the Lutheran Church in America.

So there really was no reason to think about early retirement except the nagging question, Do I want to spend my entire working life with one company? The answer was always no. I shared my concerns with Judith frequently until it appeared time to do something about them.

A friend had given me high recommendations for a career-counseling center in another city. I secured more information about their services and signed a contract with them. The career-counseling center dealt primarily with persons who were unhappy in their jobs and needed a change. The director of the center was intrigued to be working with a person who was happy and successful in his job but felt he needed to make a change. Judith was also involved in the counseling. Spouses need to be part of such a process.

A few weeks before our appointment, we received a thick package from the center containing a variety of tests to complete and mail back. We also received a detailed financial question-naire and we both had to complete detailed medical histories.

By the time we arrived for our first day, the staff of four already had a good knowledge of us. The director was warm and friendly. He explained the kind of tests we would receive and what we could expect of the center at the end of the process. He said that he and his associates wanted to test my reasons for desiring a change when everything in my life seemed to be going so well.

For three solid days we were given individual batteries of psychological and intelligence tests. We received full medical exams at a nearby hospital. We were done each day by about 4:30 P.M. and had the rest of the evening to ourselves. A nearby hotel was our home away from home.

The staff kept prodding me to determine why I wanted to change. One of the questions in the preconference material was, "What are your hobbies?" I responded with jogging, golf, gardening, travel, and visiting family. There also was an essay question asking what you would like to do after retirement. I wrote that, first and foremost, I would like to give back to society for the blessings God has given me by doing volunteer work. I also wanted to spend quality time with Judith in travel, including visiting our family.

In a later interview one of the psychologists pointed out that very few hobbies appeared on my list of things I wanted to do after retirement.

"What happened to golf?" he asked pointedly.

"It takes too much time." I replied.

"People around here would give anything to belong to that Saucon Valley Country Club," he pressed. "Don't you have fun playing golf?"

"Not very much. I do it for entertaining customers."

"Well, what do you do for fun?" he persisted. "Look, today I have great fun in sailing. When I retire I want to buy a larger sailboat and spend all my time drifting in the Caribbean, soaking up the sun. What do you think of that?" He leaned back in his chair, with his arms crossed over his chest, smiling.

"I think it is a terrible waste of a life," I said quite candidly.

He was shocked. "What do you mean by that?"

"I mean you have so much experience and knowledge about psychology that it would be a shame to spend your senior years in total self-indulgence."

He paused for a moment, then continued, "But you must consider your own needs. You need to lighten up. It is not being self-indulgent to have some fun in life."

"Well, I do have fun playing with our grandchildren, traveling with Judith, and entertaining others in our home. But I also greatly enjoy being of service to others. God has given me so many blessings in my life without my earning them that there is something inside of me that wants to give to others."

I could tell that he did not expect we would be talking about religion.

He smiled and said softly, "I thought you were a Lutheran, not a Calvinist."

"I think Martin Luther would have affirmed what I just said. Besides, is it emotionally unhealthy for me to have a touch of Calvinism?"

"I guess not," he said, rising and shaking my hand.

When I told Judith about the conversation, I said, "I guess he thinks I'm a religious kook." But I just couldn't agree that spending all your senior years floating around in a sailboat is a good use of one's life.

On the morning of the fourth day, the executive director went over the results of our tests. He said the center never tells clients what they should do, but outlines possibilities to consider and possibilities to avoid. For example, one of the early options I expressed was that Judith and I could be partners in some type of business. "Bad idea," was his evaluation of that. "You have a good marriage going now. Why risk it in a joint business partnership?"

When I asked about the option of starting my own management consulting business, the director said that looked like one of my best ideas. We also discussed other possibilities.

When we left, the director suggested that I give things time to settle. "Don't decide now. Think about it and give me a call if you have any questions," he said.

I have gone into a great deal of detail on my career-counseling center experience so that readers could get a sense of what it is like. I felt it was worthwhile. One warning: good career-counseling centers do not come cheap. But they are an excellent resource for planning what to do in the senior years.

As it turned out, I decided to start a management consulting business. I made the decision at age fifty-four and set the time for leaving Bethlehem Steel for age fifty-six.

In the meantime I did two things. First, I began talking with companies and individuals who might be my first clients. Several surfaced immediately. Second, I made certain I understood what my early retirement benefits would be and I got them in writing.

For two years I had second thoughts about what I had decided to do. Each morning I awoke, eager to get to my job. I enjoyed my work immensely and the daily interaction with others was very stimulating. I was earning good money and had many executive perks. I frequently asked myself, "Why am I doing this?" But when I took the time to think through my long-term objectives, it seemed right . . . until the next morning.

As it turned out, the year after I retired in 1981, the entire steel industry started a long decline. Bethlehem Steel spun off many of its subsidiary businesses, including the division for which I was sales manager. Had I not retired when I did, I would most certainly have been a victim of corporate downsizing within a few years.

My senior living has turned out just about the way I planned it back in 1980. After I left Bethlehem Steel I did management consulting and strategic planning for two steel-producing companies, one of which was foreign. I also did planning and marketing consulting for three steel fabricating companies and served on the boards of two of them. I did planning for a steel-fabricating institute and some nonsteel companies, including an electronics company. I did some management training for the Lutheran Church in America. That led to a contract with them to do training on corporate social responsibility. I also planned and coordinated several dialogues between church and business leaders. For six years I taught a course called Religion, Ethics, and Business at one of our local colleges.

My intent to work with nonprofit organizations has led to a number of church-related assignments. I have helped to organize interfaith coalitions on poverty and on ethics in the workplace, and I am a board member of the Lehigh County Conference of Churches. The Lehigh County Housing Authority and the Community Action Committee of the Lehigh Valley are two secular nonprofits with whom I still work. I was a founding member of the Lutheran Academy and of the Coalition for Ministry in Daily Life, both international organizations for Christians trying to connect faith and daily life.

One of my main interests since my retirement from Bethlehem Steel has been finding ways to connect one's Sunday world with the weekday world of work. I have had seven books published on this topic and, as a consequence, have been called upon for conferences, leadership, and teaching all over the United States.

During all the years I was developing new senior activities and ministries, Judith was busy doing the same in her own style. Here is her story.

Judith's Story

Retirement for me has never existed. As a female child of the Depression, society's and my expectations for adulthood and old age, regardless of ability, were low. I could marry well and have a family. That was the first and best option. With a college degree I could be a teacher, social worker, lab technician, or an educated mother. I could train for secretarial work or nursing. Most other professions were effectively closed to women, or the barriers so difficult to break that only the hardiest hurdled the "no women allowed" strictures.

My life has been a series of stages: childhood, teenage, college, marriage and parenthood, and self-actualization. The last began in my middle forties with our move from Devon to Allentown, our hometown. It was for me a step backward in time and place.

I spent a weekend crying. Even though I was Mrs. William E. Diehl and the mother of Shelley, Bill, Buffy, and Jennifer, I did have some identity of my own, or at least I thought I did. I really did not want to resume my old friendships and my old status as a daughter and sister and aunt as if I had not been gone for many years and matured and changed. I knew I would be stifled by the expectations others had of me.

Our son Bill and daughter Shelley were in college. Buffy and Jennifer were old enough that they did not need me to be a full-time stay-at-home mom. And Bill's mother, Grandee, who moved along with us, expected that I would play bridge, dine at the country club, maybe play some golf, and live the life of leisure expected of the wife of a successful steel executive.

Rejecting in my mind the notion of the leisure life, my game plan, although loosely constructed, was to explore all the options available to women at that time. A closet feminist, I eagerly responded to the plethora of opportunities suddenly opening, thanks to the feminist movement.

Shelley, in the fear that I would waste my brains and be bored, pushed me into going to graduate school at Lehigh University. I loved all my classes and did well. But the time came for me to do practice teaching. I really don't like to teach, especially high school students. End of graduate school.

An old friend talked me into joining the League of Women Voters. It seemed like a good way to meet new women and keep my brain in gear. The League had an observer corps made up of members who were willing to attend the meetings of school boards, township commissioners or supervisors, county commissioners, city councils, and borough councils.

I volunteered to watch and report back to the League what the Lower Macungie Township supervisors were doing. With knitting in hand I attended the twice-monthly meetings. Usually I was the only member of the public present.

I remember asking to see the township annual budget. I had to go to the home of one of the supervisors to see it. He told me I was the first person who was ever interested.

After about six months of attending the township supervisors' meetings as the League's observer, the three supervisors decided, with prodding from their solicitor, that they needed to form a parks and recreation board. The township was growing fast, and open space and recreation might become a problem if they failed to plan ahead. They decided, too, that this board should have some women members. "But we don't know any women," one supervisor protested. Then they looked out at me, the lone member of the public sitting there, surrounded by empty seats. I was named to the board.

To continue my search for new challenges, I rejoined the American Association of University Women (AAUW) after a twenty-year hiatus. Along with the usual study groups there was a one-year special project: Project PRY (Protection of the Rights of Youth). I became the state coordinator and sat on the state board.

As part of this project, our local study group investigated the county juvenile justice system. We discovered early on that our juvenile detention facility held many kids who were truants. But there was no schooling provided for them in the thirty to sixty days they were held. It seemed pretty silly to us. We found a teacher and convinced the juvenile probation people to provide the funds to pay her.

Next, I couldn't turn down an old friend's request that I become part of a new group, started by a woman probation officer, called Volunteer Friends for Girls on Probation. Members of the group were all active churchwomen. I was immediately assigned a probationer named Sissie who was seventeen years old. We met once a week for lunch. I think I was the only dependable woman she had in her life.

When Sissie turned eighteen, no longer a juvenile in the eyes of the court, I saw her infrequently. By the time she was nineteen she had a baby and had spent several months in jail as an accessory to an armed robbery attempt. She asked Bill and me to be godparents of her baby. We also were the guests of honor at her wedding—we sat at the head table with the bridal party.

Sissie is now fifty years old. Sometimes several years pass before I hear from her. When she calls me now she is usually looking for help with her three grown sons and several grandchildren. Her sons, starting when they were juveniles, have been in ongoing and increasingly serious trouble. I do what I can to help and support her.

The 1970s were exciting but fearful times for women, especially those of my mother's generation and my own. In the search for equality, the women's movement turned upside down our long-held societal concepts of the roles and expectations of women. Many older women felt terribly threatened, as did the majority of men.

As one thing led to another and as doors opened for me and to other women, I started to worry about the quality of life for girls and women less fortunate than myself. The issue of how women were treated in the criminal justice system became my concern when I was part of a group of AAUW women who wangled a tour of the women's section of Lehigh County prison.

We were appalled and outraged at what we saw. It was unfit for human habitation, and yet there were fifteen women in twelve 4 feet x 7 feet barred cells. Male guards smirked at us. The tension was palpable. We formed a coalition of twenty church and women's organizations with the long name of Citizens' Coalition for a Women's Prison Annex. It took us five years of pushing and cajoling the county until we got a new unit built for incarcerated women.

This next opportunity came as a result of my church involvement and interest in women's issues. A forward-looking bishop of the Northeast Pennsylvania (NEPA) synod of the Lutheran Church in America asked me to be on a newly created synod committee called the Changing Roles of Women and Men in Church and Society.

Our initial task was to educate ourselves about the roles of women in the Bible with emphasis on new understandings and interpretations. Instead of the old sources, we read some works of women theologians. A professor of Old Testament spoke to us several times. He prefaced his talks with the admission that he had revised his interpretations and class lectures with the advent of women students in the seminary. They challenged him to reexamine the biblical texts with a focus on the roles and significance of the women in the texts. For the first time in my life, in my late forties, I realized I was not a second-class Christian. I actually cried with joy.

As the women's movement gathered steam, increasing numbers of organizations searched for women to serve on previously all-male boards. A social worker who was a member of our church support group proffered my name for the Health Systems Council of Eastern Pennsylvania.

These councils, established in the mid-1970s throughout the United States were federally funded. They had broad powers to approve or deny new construction and equipment in their regions. Increasing the numbers of hospital beds, CT scanners, nursing homes, as well as the establishment of HMOs all came before the councils for review and vote. It was an attempt by the federal government to contain runaway health costs. To some extent, it was successful.

In the end, though, this exercise in trying to curb health costs became too political. When the hospitals turned nasty, some council members were threatened with job loss. One, whose son was about to graduate from a local college, was told his son might not graduate if he did not vote in favor of a hospital project. Doctors, nurses, and hospital administrators tried persuasion and intimidation. But I was reassured in that there was no way my job could be threatened. I didn't hold one. Being "only a housewife" finally had its advantages.

My only political involvement prior to my joining the League of Women Voters was voting on a regular basis. The league changed all that. The League had embarked on a long study of the existing three-commissioner form of county government in Pennsylvania. The consensus reached by the League was that this form was antiquated and needed to be changed.

The Pennsylvania legislature in 1972 enacted a law allowing townships and counties to form, through the election process, government study commissions that would meet and then report back to the voters with recommendations for change or no change in the form of government.

With continuing pressure from the local League, the three Lehigh County commissioners agreed to put the question of a government study on the ballot. At the same time, the voters would choose eleven members for a study commission. The voters said yes to the study commission, and I won a seat on it.

A year and a half later when the government study commission's recommendation of change was accepted, I ran for a seat on the new legislative body and lost. I was elected to the Lehigh County Council two years later. A firm believer in limited terms for everyone from the president on down, I served only two terms.

I experienced some unexpected and gratifying consequences from my foray into elected office. A trailblazer in local politics, I served as a role model and mentor for younger women who wanted to follow. I gained women friends, some the ages of our daughters, who supported me and worked for my elections. I was the "token" woman cochair on election campaigns for several men running for judgeships. I also cochaired the successful campaign of the first woman elected to the bench of Common Pleas Court in Lehigh County.

In another area, my most satisfying endeavor involved a piano teacher friend who had a dream. Since her early days of working to pay for expensive piano lessons, she envisioned a music school where everyone with an interest could receive quality music education without regard to their ability to pay. I worked with Martha to turn her dream into reality. My contribution was to put together a governing board that was not only committed to the concept, but was willing to work to garner community support.

Moving through the 1970s, '80s, and '90s, I realized how important my given name was in carving out my own space as an individual. I use Judith Ruhe Diehl now instead of Mrs. William E. Diehl. When a woman takes on her husband's name, she can become invisible culturally and socially. I don't enjoy invisibility.

Where am I presently? I continue my memberships in the League of Women Voters and the American Association of University Women. Both groups currently suffer from having too many aging members like me, and not enough younger women joining.

Our Citizens' Coalition for a Women's Prison Annex, after it was successful in getting livable quarters for the women in the county jail, brought in the PROGRAM for Female Offenders, now known as the PROGRAM for Women and Families. The agency deals with women involved in the justice system along with their children and spouses or boyfriends and other family members. It runs the women's work release center for the jail. I sit on its board of directors.

Sissie has moved out of my life, temporarily I'm sure, and I now am working with a nineteen-year-old single mother with two-year-old twins. This single mom, caught in the welfare-to-work morass, needs all the help and then some from our church team, part of the Relational Sponsorship initiative.

Together, Bill and I are active in our church's seniors' group, the Relational Sponsorship program, and Meals-on-Wheels.

My particular and ongoing passion, which grew out of my membership in the synod committee, is the urgent need, for the sake of all women and girls, to change the male language of the Bible and the church to inclusive language. Given the entrenched traditions and mindset of the church, it is an almost hopeless task. As a woman equally created in the image of God, I take small comfort in the fact that I am not called to be successful. I am called only to be faithful. So I will continue to chip away at the encrustations of male language and tradition, and hope that I have made a small dent.

Other Stories

There you have, in rather great detail, two quite different stories about planning and moving into post-retirement senior living. I have spoken with many persons who have recently retired from their life's work or who are about to do so. Not many did any specific planning.

One close friend of mine, a college professor, has just moved into his years of senior living. "I wished I had done some planning," he confided recently. I asked him what had kept him from doing so. "Well," his voice drifted off, "I guess I never thought about it." That is very typical of many people with whom I chatted. So they have ended up doing "Honey-do" chores around the house. "Honey, do this" and "Honey, do that." Most of them are unhappy in this role.

Another close friend, who will retire from his law practice a year from now, said he had two offers for postretirement living. One was to read for books on tape; the other was to do voiceovers for commercial television ads. He got these offers because he has a clear and distinctive voice. "I don't know if I'll take one or the other or both," he said. He was pleased that the offers came to him rather than having to go out and look for things to do.

"Have you ever done some serious planning for your post-retirement years?" I asked.

"No," he said, "but things will come to me, I'm sure."

Another friend of mine, a dentist, recently decided it was time to retire. "I was getting tired of my work and many of my long-term patients were dying," he explained.

"What are you doing?" I asked.

"Oh, I've been puttering around the house and one day a week I volunteer to deliver mail at the hospital."

"How is it going with you?" I inquired.

"I'm bored to death and don't know what to do about it."

He never planned for life after retirement.

One former neighbor of ours has recently retired as the head of the department of gynecology at our local hospital. We ran into him at a public event recently. I asked him what he was up to.

"Oh, mowing lawns," he replied with a big grin.

"Mowing lawns? How can that keep you busy?"

"We have a huge lawn, as you know, and our daughter has a large one also."

I bit my tongue. Here was a highly educated professional who had devoted almost every waking hour to his work and never had any outside interests that might be of use to him in retirement except mowing lawns.

I find that most people have not done planning for post-retirement living for one reason: denial. Emotionally, retirement from our primary work puts us one step closer to death. And while we all know, rationally, that we will die someday, emotionally we do not want to think about it. Since retirement is drawing us closer to death, we postpone planning for our senior living until later.

Also, work is so much a part of who we are culturally, some may feel dislocated socially upon retirement.

Ministry in Senior Living

"The Holy Spirit Empowers Us for Ministry in Daily Life"—that motto is found on every piece of printed material coming out of our church office. Every letter, every envelope has it. Every Sunday bulletin, every church directory has it. The coffee mugs we use on Sundays, at meeting nights, and for dinners carry it.

As a congregation, we work hard to help all our members see themselves as ministers. Yes, *ministers*. Our Sunday bulletins emphasize the point in the listing of the congregation roster:

Ministers: All the Members of the Congregation
Pastors: The Rev. Al Roberts and the Rev. Suzanne Macfadden

The word *minister* has been badly misused in our everyday language. My *Random House* dictionary indicates that the noun *minister* means "a person authorized to conduct religious worship; clergyman, pastor." Succeeding definitions speak of "a person appointed to some high office of the state" and "a diplomatic representative" and "a person acting as the agent or instrument of another." Yet the verb means "to give service, care or aid."[1] Based on the meaning of the verb *minister,* wouldn't one expect that the first noun definition would be "one who gives service, care or aid"?

In the New Testament there are numerous verses in which Jesus ministered to the needs of others and verses where the angels ministered to him. The epistles have a number of references to early believers ministering to one another.

Some people mistakenly believe that laypersons minister to each other solely within their church. Not so. Christians minister primarily in and to the world—in their occupations, their families, their communities, and in the church.

The word *priest* also has biblical and theological significance for all believers. Reference to a "kingdom of priests," meaning all the people, can be found in both the Old and New Testaments.

When Moses went up Mount Sinai, God told him:

Thus you shall say to the house of Jacob, and tell the Israelites: You have seen what I did to the Egyptians, and how I bore you on eagles' wings and brought you to myself. Now therefore, if you obey my voice and keep my covenant, you shall be my treasured possession out of all the peoples. Indeed, the whole earth is mine, but you shall be for me a priestly kingdom and a holy nation. These are the words that you shall speak to the Israelites. (Exod. 19:3-6)

In Isaiah 61, frequently called the "good news of deliverance" chapter, we read: "You shall be called priests of the Lord, you shall be named ministers of our God" (Isa. 61:6). The identification of all the people being part of a priesthood is picked up again in 1 Peter 2:9-10: "You are a chosen race, a royal priesthood, a holy nation, God's own people, in order that you may proclaim the mighty acts of him who called you out of darkness into his marvelous light. Once you were not a people, but now you are God's people."

The salutation in the Revelation to John contains the words, "To him who loves us and freed us from our sins by his blood, and made us to be a kingdom, priests serving his God and Father, to him be glory and dominion forever and ever. Amen" (Rev. 1:5b-6).

It is Martin Luther who is given credit for the doctrine of a universal ministry of the baptized, more commonly known as the priesthood of all believers. At our baptism, Luther argued, we were all called into a universal priesthood. He maintained that if you have been baptized, you have been ordained into the priesthood. There were no hierarchies of priesthood among the believers. He said, "The housemaid on her knees scrubbing the floor is doing a work as pleasing in the eyes of God as the priest on his knees before the altar saying the mass." It was a radical statement in Luther's time and still is today. But he meant it. No hierarchy. All ministry is equally pleasing in the eyes of God—bishop and broker, pastor and plumber, deacon and doctor, nun and nanny, monk and mail carrier, friar and firefighter, house builder and homemaker. All are equally pleasing in the eyes of God.

Ministry in daily life has no termination clause. We do not put our ministries on the shelf when the day of retirement comes. Christian ministry is a lifelong calling. While it may take different forms as we grow older, it is always before us.

In my book *The Monday Connection*,[2] I outlined five styles of ministry that made sense to me in my working life. They were (1) doing my work with competency, (2) bringing my faith into the presence of those with whom I interact, (3) being ethical, (4) striving for change, and (5) following a simple lifestyle. Those five styles are as relevant to the ministries of my senior living as they were to my full-time working years. More about them in chapter 6.

It is important, as we plan our senior living, that we carefully evaluate our values and talents to find the ministries that will be most appropriate for us. Nicolas Coni, William Davison, and Stephen Webster, in their authoritative book, *Aging: The Facts*, argue that planning for retirement cannot start too soon.[3]

My lawyer friend may decide that taping books and lending his voice to commercials are the best ministries for him, but I wonder if the years of law experience might be of greater service to poor people who cannot afford legal services. Has he considered that?

And my dentist friend, who is bored stiff—does he realize that there are almost no dentists in our area who will take Medicaid patients? Could he do something about that?

In a later chapter we will offer a wide variety of ministries for senior living. But remember, there is no termination clause for Christian ministry in daily life. It ain't over till it's over. For that reason we should actively consider how we can best use our God-given talents as we move into senior living.

chapter
four
to move
or not
to move

In the previous chapter on planning for senior living, no mention was made about where to live. In some instances the plan itself will dictate moving to some other location, as in the case of wanting to move to Florida or Arizona for health reasons.

But in most instances one's plan for senior living can be carried out without moving. A postretirement job, volunteering, travel, and more education are elements of plans that would not require a move from one's home; however, the style of living as we move through the senior years may change. Do we want to stay in our home until we die? Large numbers of people do. Do we want to move into smaller accommodations when the children have all moved out? Many do. Do we want to get rid of lawn and garden maintenance, snow removal, house repairs, and similar homeowner necessities as we age? Many do. Are we interested in continuing care-retirement communities? Again, many people are.

This chapter will deal with style of living as far as housing is concerned. Many studies have shown that a fear of dying in some impersonal institution causes seven out of ten people to say that they want to die at home. But where is home? For some, like Aunt Elsie, it is that place where one has lived most of life. That is the way Judith's mother saw it also. In this chapter, we will look at their stories and other stories as we examine the issues surrounding choosing a living arrangement.

My Aunt Elsie was the elder of my mother's two sisters. She never married. The whispered story in our family was that her true love was killed in World War I, but that was never openly acknowledged by her. She lived with my grandparents all her life. Her income, when added to that of my grandfather, enabled the family of three to buy a nice house in western Allentown and pay off the mortgage in twenty years.

When my grandmother became too feeble to cook and do laundry, it was my grandfather, who had been retired from his job, who took care of her. Aunt Elsie was still working but she helped by paying to have an inclinator installed on the rear stairway of their three-bedroom home. When "Nana Yellis" died at age eighty-nine, Aunt Elsie was sixty-seven and still working.

Aunt Elsie was retired from her job at age seventy and stayed at home with my grandfather for two years until he died at ninety-five. She lived alone in the house for eighteen more years until her death at age ninety-two.

Elsie was fiercely independent and vowed to die in her own home. But as she aged, she gradually needed to depend on others to take care of her everyday needs, such as transportation, shopping, and putting out the trash. As her ability to walk diminished, she needed a walker.

Her health began to fail around age ninety and she had frequent hospital stays. Her doctor recommended she go to a skilled nursing facility, to which she responded with a strong "Never!" Finally, one episode in the hospital was so serious that her doctor refused to discharge her to her home. Since my mother and I were her closest family, the doctor told us what had to be done. And although we had no power of attorney, we agreed.

The day came for her transfer to a skilled nursing facility. She appealed to the doctor and to my mother and me. We all said it was in her best interests. When the ambulance personnel arrived, she closed her eyes and refused to talk. I spoke to her but she would not answer.

When she got to the skilled nursing facility, she kept her eyes shut, said nothing, and refused medications, water, and food. I tried to get her to respond to me, but she would not. After three days she was dead.

Judith's Mother

My mother was a suffragette and rebel when she married my father. Ambitious and bright, she landed a real catch in my father, a college graduate and editor of a daily newspaper. My father, a somewhat enlightened Victorian male, allowed and encouraged my mother to continue her suffragette activities. With the sky as the limit, she planned to produce ten superior sons and no daughters. Daughters were too difficult to raise, she said. Her first child was a girl. Then came six boys. I was the seventh "son." And there was one younger boy to complete the family.

In my years growing up, Mother doted on her sons, all of whom she expected to be leaders of men, but she felt sorry for her daughters. "When you're a girl, you have to learn to take it," she warned. Her expectations for my sister and me were that we would find good husbands, as she had. She knew where the power lay.

This small biographical glimpse of my mother, this complex and opinionated woman, points up the irony of my position during the ten years after my father's death. When my father died, Mother was left with a row home in Allentown and a non-working farm on a hillside ten miles away. Her sources of income were a small pension from the newspaper and Social Security. The care of my mother and the farm and the row home now fell to me. Even though I had five living brothers and a sister, I was the only sibling living in the state of Pennsylvania.

The row house was convenient and cozy during the cold months of the year, but Mother never considered it her real home. Her love was the farm with its land and trees and lawn and flowers. Its isolation from neighbors added to its appeal.

In the beginning, Mother moved to the farm by the middle of May and back to the city the end of October. As the years passed, she left the city by Memorial Day and returned after Labor Day.

During the summer months, Mother was adequately cared for by a stream of grandchildren. Of twenty, there were always several who could be counted on to spend most of their summer at the farm. As Mother needed more help bathing and dressing, her long-time neighbors, Annie and Mike, appeared weekly at the farm—Mike to do odd jobs and Annie to assist Mother.

Early on, a grandson fresh out of college lived with Mother year round while he worked as a reporter on the daily newspaper. This took care of one winter out of ten. The remaining nine were increasingly difficult and challenging.

Our family—Bill and I and our four children plus Bill's mother—lived in Devon, a suburb of Philadelphia. The trip to Allentown was exactly one hour. At least once a week I drove to Allentown with Bill's mother; I to see and care for my mother, and Bill's mother to visit her sister, Aunt Elsie, who lived alone in their family home.

As Mother aged, there was a role reversal. Mother, always in charge, needed help with her bills and checkbook, with her shopping and her medications. She became increasingly helpless physically and mentally. She grudgingly gave me her power of attorney. But she fought me every step of the way as I made more of the decisions affecting her life.

She needed help in the kitchen and company during the day. I searched long and hard to find a part-time companion and finally hired a woman. After the third day, Mother fired her. Back to square one. Repeated twice, I finally had to concede that Mother would not accept a stranger in her home. The high school age son of a friend agreed to spend time and run errands for Mother after school. He was faithful and Mother liked him very much. But she decided she would not pay him because he was too young. I had to write checks to him myself.

Mother did have a wonderful neighbor next door at her Allentown home who shopped for her, occasionally ate with her, and looked in on her daily. Without this attention, Mother would not have been able to survive.

Why did I spend so much time and effort on my mother, besides the given that women in our society are the caretakers? Like most of the people of her generation, she felt that moving to a nursing home was out of the question. "Don't you ever put me in a nursing home. I'll die." She was adamant: she expected to be cared for by her family, and this was the way it was. With financial help from my brothers and sister, we could have managed the cost of a retirement home. That was never the issue.

In fact, Mother fell and cracked her pelvis one Sunday morning. After a few days of hospitalization, she was moved to a nursing home to recuperate. I expected she would spend her remaining years there, but I was mistaken. She hated the place. She called me one day after several weeks and ordered, "Come and get me." I, the obedient daughter, picked her up and drove her back to her Allentown home. She walked slowly and with a cane. To this day, I do not know if she was in terrible pain as she walked. She refused further X-rays and she continued to walk until her final day.

I could never come to terms with this role reversal in my relationship with my mother. This strong, opinionated woman became a physically and emotionally frail person. The transformation meant that I had to tell my mother what to do after a lifetime of her telling me how I should live every aspect of my life. And Mother struggled against my assuming any leadership. Much of our time together was spent wrangling over small things.

A week before Labor Day in the tenth summer after my father died, Mother knew we would soon move her back to Allentown for the winter. Grandchildren had to return to school; tenants would be moving into the farm for the winter months.

Looking back, I see that Mother couldn't face the struggle of another lonely winter in the city. That Monday, at the farm, as Annie was helping Mother with her bath, Mother said, "Don't tell anyone. I stopped taking my medicines." Annie said nothing. Two days later, Mother died. She was ready.

The Human Cost of Dying at Home

In Aunt Elsie's case, despite her valiant efforts, it was not possible for her to die at home. Her doctor's decision forced her to go to an institution—the thing she dreaded most. Judith's mother was able to realize her wish to die at home, but only with the help of many friends and her devoted daughter who weekly drove the hundred-mile round trip to check on her. Judith's mother expected that her family and friends would care for her. So did most of the people of that generation.

To illustrate, here are a few notes on Christmas cards we received last December.

Dot wrote from Greensboro, North Carolina, "My mother, at ninety-three, is still in her home with around-the-clock care. I spend a lot of time going back and forth."

Barbara, who lives in suburban Washington, D.C., about 150 miles from her aged parents, wrote, "I have been going to Pennsylvania at least two to three weekends a month, helping with chores, and serving as a social worker, trying to connect all the messages to and from the various doctors."

Louise, a widow about our age who lives alone within twenty minutes time of a son and daughter, wrote "I had a nasty fall on a broken sidewalk on August 17, putting me in the hospital until August 22. Then going to a nursing home for therapy until October 23. Back in my own home now." What she did not say was that it was her son and daughter who took her to and from her daily therapy between August and October.

Jeff and Doris, both age fifty-three, almost had their marriage end due to caring for Jeff's parents. Every weekend Jeff was gone to be with his eighty-six-year-old parents. The five-day-a-week live-in caretaker he and Doris had secured for the parents was not on duty. His weekly absence took a toll on his marriage of thirty-three years. "My wife and I started off working as a team," says Jeff, "but gradually she became more distant, a little more resentful of the parents and jealous of the time I spent with them."[1]

Life can be especially stressful for the "sandwich generation"; that is, those who are caregivers for both their parents and their children at the same time. Naturally, there is a strong emotional tie to one's home. It is, after all, the place where we have lived most of our life. It would be nice to be able to spend our last years there and to die there. But in trying to do so there is often a high cost to be paid by the ones we love most—our family.

Much as one might like to stay in one's home until death, the reality is that very few of us can do so without assistance. The older we get, the more we must rely on others; frequently, family members. Do we really want to do this to our children?

Bill's Mother

Is there another way? Here's the story of my mother.

My mother, having been abandoned by my father when I was young, lived alone for much of her life. She had a job with an automobile finance company and made enough money to live independently in a nice apartment. I was her only child, "the only thing she had." She retired from her job with a small pension. But even with Social Security added in, it was not enough for her to live on. I had to help in some way, keeping in mind that she was an independent person.

We were living in Devon, some fifty miles away. Although she was still healthy and active, I persuaded her to come live with us. When she agreed, I added an apartment to our house. It consisted of a living room, a bedroom, and a bath. Since she had some money in a savings account, I agreed to let her pay for some of the construction and we agreed she would pay us a small rent.

Our two youngest daughters grew attached to "Grandee." She was our permanent sitter whenever we went out. She joined our church and developed some close friends of her own. That was the positive side of living with us. Judith feels that the negative side was, simply put, the presence of another woman in the house. It was an experience of one generation looking over the shoulder of the next, and sitting in judgment. "To be more specific," says Judith, "Grandee, a lovely and gentle woman, was rigid in her thinking and hated change of any kind. Applied to the food I prepared, the child-raising methods I employed, the way I interacted with Bill, and the nontraditional paths I was taking, Grandee was, for the twenty-three years she lived with us, subtly critical of me. She and I engaged in a subtle tug of war in which Bill and the children were the rope. It was difficult for both of us, and it continued far too long." I completely understood Judith's feelings, but what else could we do?

I was transferred to the Bethlehem Steel home office in 1969 and we built a new, large house in Allentown with a slightly larger apartment for Grandee. She developed Parkinson's disease. Over the years, she became more disabled. She became more dependent upon us and began to feel she was a burden.

When Aunt Elsie died, she left her estate to her two sisters. My mother got a nice sum of money. "Now I want to go to Luther Crest," Mother said as soon as she had the money. She did not want to become totally dependent upon us as her physical condition worsened.

At the Luther Crest nursing facility, she had a private room where she could have some of her favorite furniture and wall art. She had her meals in a dining room until she could no longer make the trip there. Meals were then delivered to her room at her favorite chair.

I visited her about every other day. In her early years there, we were able to take her to our home for Christmas, Easter, and other special occasions. Eventually, she was totally confined to her room.

Whenever our children would visit with their babies and growing children, they always visited Grandee, which made it a special day for her. She was always very friendly and cooperative with the nurses. They truly loved her.

After about four years at Luther Crest, her money was gone. I expected that I would be asked to take over her payments, but instead received a pleasant surprise.

"Our policy is to keep our residents in their same living conditions once they have been here for two years," I was told.

And therein lies the advantage of being at a church-related facility. Most of the for-profit nursing homes will turn people out. Most nonprofit church-related nursing homes will keep their patients even if all their financial assets are gone. For my mother, Luther Crest depended upon her Social Security, Medicaid reimbursements, and earnings from a Luther Crest endowment fund to cover her expenses.

My mother's Parkinson's disease kept getting worse. She died on her ninety-ninth birthday. To this day, nurses who knew her remark to me what a wonderful, kind person she was.

In living with us and steadily becoming more dependent upon us, my mother saw she could not stay in her home without exacting a high cost from her family. So she made the decision to move into an institution where she would get expert care. The important element is that it was *her* decision, not ours.

The People We Feed

Judith and I have been driving Meals-on-Wheels on the same route weekly for over five years. She drives, I deliver. We average fourteen deliveries each day that we participate.

Four of our clients live in the same apartment building, owned and operated by a local housing authority. Their apartments consist of a living room, dinette, small kitchen, bathroom, and bedroom. The building and apartments are clean and well maintained. The four residents live independently. All of them are receiving some sort of medical attention—I can tell from the number of prescriptions neatly lined up on their tables or counters. There is some degree of community life since neighbors seem to know each other, and group activities are offered.

We also deliver meals into the homes of five elderly women living independently. They live in old two-story houses, always on the first floor, usually in a single room with a bed. They have large kitchens and usually a downstairs bathroom, although two of them use portable commodes. Their rooms smell of bodily wastes. Three of them have boxes, newspapers, and unlaundered clothing piled everywhere. The other two give evidence of a weekly visit of a housekeeper. As I place the meals on the kitchen tables, I usually see from five to ten prescription bottles strewn around. How they can possibly take their medications properly is beyond me.

All of the people we visit are lonely. They would like me to sit and talk with them, but I have to remind them that others are waiting for their food. But the five women living alone in their two-story homes seem most desperate for company.

One must be careful about generalizing, but it has been my observation that the dream of independent living works best for the individual and his or her family if it takes place within a community of persons with similar needs and interests.

We have a close friend, Martin Trueblood, who has given his second career to building and managing retirement communities for the Quaker community. He agrees with my observation but confesses that he knows of no studies that have been made to prove it. Martin also makes another assertion that is important. He says that the people who make the best transition into retirement communities are those who make decisions before others have to make them for them.

Life at a Retirement Community

We have practiced Martin Trueblood's advice to make changes before we had to. When we moved from Devon to Allentown, we built a large five-bedroom colonial home with an attached apartment for my mother. When she went to the nursing home and after our youngest two daughters left home, we decided to downsize.

We sold our large home, got rid of much furniture, and moved into a ranch-style house with four bedrooms. In doing so, we made one mistake. We paid little attention to the size of the lawn and the many gardens put in by the previous owner. It did not take long for us to realize that while we downsized our housing, we upsized our landscaping and gardens. We were simply spending too much time and money working on our gardens and lawn. That fact encouraged us to move to a full-care retirement community sooner than we might have otherwise.

Luther Crest, in Allentown, Pennsylvania, is a continuing-care retirement community (CCRC). CCRCs offer a continuum of senior living on the campus. In many CCRCs, especially the newer ones, independent living units are similar to condominium apartments. Many offer home health care in the independent living apartments with visiting nurses making scheduled visits. CCRCs also have assisted-living units and skilled nursing facilities on the premises.

Luther Crest, about five miles from our previous home, consists of four three-story apartment buildings with units of various sizes and configurations. There are 260 independent living apartments in all. Judith insisted that we have a first-floor unit, and we agreed upon a "deluxe double." We have one large master bedroom, a smaller guest bedroom, two bathrooms, a large kitchen, a large open living room/dining room space, a small office for me, a laundry room, and four large walk-in closets. We have two patios, each leading out to a modest perennial garden that we planted. Pets are allowed, but we have none.

We have no lawn mowing, no snow shoveling, and no maintenance whatsoever. The unit is cleaned thoroughly every two weeks. Our contract provides for one meal per day in a large dining room, and the food there is good. Every day there are six main-course entrees from which to select. There is also a luncheon menu for those who prefer lighter fare.

There is also a bistro where residents can have meals in a less formal atmosphere. The menu is an abbreviated version of that found in the formal dining room. In warmer weather, the bistro customers can eat on a large patio at tables.

Our contract provides for comprehensive care. When we begin to have health problems, we can have a nurse visit our apartment. If we become completely unable to care for our daily routines, we can move to an assisted-living unit in an adjoining wing. Each assisted-living apartment features one large living or sleeping room with private bath. Assistance with eating, dressing, toilet, bath, and mobility (a minimum of any three) is provided by trained staff. A registered nurse is available around the clock. Meals are taken in a special dining room or delivered to a resident's room, depending upon mobility. When full-time nursing care is necessary, residents move to another floor of the same building. The nursing unit is actually four wings radiating from a central nurses' station. One wing is devoted to residents with Alzheimer's disease. All wings have both single and double bedrooms. Physicians are present every day and are on call around the clock. Registered nurses are on duty twenty-four hours a day, seven days a week.

Luther Crest residents can secure the services of visiting nurses in their apartments, just as they would in their former homes. Furthermore, if the time comes for hospice care (see chapter 10), they can move back into their apartment from a hospital or from nursing care, just as they would in their former home.

Despite the fact that we can come and go as we please, there is a bit of an institutional flavor to Luther Crest (as there is for most retirement communities, I am sure). The ages of the residents varies from late sixties to late nineties. Many of the residents are women who have outlived their husbands and whose mobility is somewhat limited. For various reasons, they have given up driving their cars. They spend most of their time on the Luther Crest campus. If they need a ride to see a doctor, or to the grocery store, or to a cultural event, they have available one of Luther Crest's three vans or the station wagon. A full-time activities person provides opportunities for residents to take bus trips to local music or drama events, or to enjoy in-house activities such as movies, dances, church, card games, speakers, musical groups, and bingo. In the commons area of independent living, there is a large assembly room for Sunday worship services and weekday resident meetings, parties, dances, movies, and musical events. There is a library, a gift shop, a bank, a mailroom, and a small private dining room for special events. The mailroom has two large bulletin boards that carry announcements of upcoming events and the arrival of new residents. We have our own internal television station that posts schedules for the week, daily menus, and other items of interest.

On the lower level is a beauty shop, doctors' offices, an exercise room, a poolroom, and a large woodworking shop where all tools are held in common. There is a computer schoolroom where residents can learn to become computer literate. Volunteer instructors help with computer problems.

Judith and I participate in some of the Luther Crest activities but, because we moved from a home only five miles away, most of our social life and all of our volunteer work continues to be in the outside world and in our church. We still have two cars and use them both almost every day. I am sure that as we get older and our mobility becomes more limited, we will be more involved in Luther Crest social life.

Perhaps the biggest emotional loss for me is the family Christmas gathering we always had in our home. We used to be able to sleep eighteen family members (with kids in sleeping bags on the floor) in our previous homes. That is impossible at Luther Crest. Our eldest daughter, Shelley, has eagerly taken over the role of being family matriarch and hosting us all at her large home in Connecticut, right on Long Island Sound. But I still miss having family Christmas in our own home.

Obviously, not everyone can afford a full-scale retirement community. My experience on our county housing authority, however, has convinced me that no citizen needs to live in the rundown, cluttered, smelly conditions that I see every time I deliver Meals-on-Wheels. Better options are available for those with fewer resources.

Making Decisions

An excellent resource for considering various types of retirement communities for yourself or a loved one is the *Consumer Reports Complete Guide to Health Services for Seniors.*[2] (An extract from the book—"Is Assisted Living the Right Choice?"—can be found in the January 2001 issue of *Consumer Reports.*)

Another resource is the American Association of Homes and Services for the Aging, a nationwide nonprofit association of about 5,000 facilities for the aging. They can be contacted by phone at (202) 783-2242, or by visiting their Web site at www.aahsa.org. The Web site includes a searchable directory of its members.

Until recently, the pattern for senior residential living was to go from a large house to a condominium with all its amenities, and then to a retirement community. The newer retirement communities are providing such condo-style housing that people are going directly from their homes into a modern "active-adult" community (even the builders are dropping the word *retirement*). These communities have all the services of full-care retirement communities, but provide many more amenities for active adults. They include indoor and outdoor swimming pools, tennis courts, walking or jogging paths, bike lanes, fitness rooms, sauna, and clubhouses. Sun City, Arizona, is the granddaddy of "age-qualified" senior living. Developed by Del Webb in 1960, Sun City has mushroomed over the years. Originally geared to the Social Security beneficiary, the newer Sun City homes have shifted to a resort-type environment.

The Del Webb organization is well aware of the reasons some people will not move to Sun City, Arizona, for their senior years. And guess what? They are bringing Sun City amenities to the North. In 1999, Del Webb opened Sun City Huntley, a small town forty-five miles from downtown Chicago. Del Webb is not alone in this approach to seniors. Builders are breaking ground where people have spent their working lives and where ties to family, friends, and community are strongest. Sun City Huntley is set on 2,156 acres with a golf course and a 94,000-square-foot lodge that houses fitness and recreational activities. One of the first families to move in was Dean Whitfield, age seventy, and his wife, Shirley. Why? All of the couple's twenty grandchildren live within thirty miles of them.[3]

A similar but smaller community has been built in Warwick, New York, which is aimed at the fifty-five-and-older market. The project is the baby of Steve Mann, a forty-eight-year-old developer who made his living building large suburban homes. He says, "We have never had a response like this for anything we have tried. We have 500 people on our waiting list."[4]

The point is that the distinctions between the so-called retirement communities and the modern-age-qualified condominium communities are fast disappearing.[5] The result is that baby boomers are beginning to move into upscale senior living communities in increasing numbers. "With 76 million boomers out there—many just starting to hit retirement age—marketing to a younger generation just made economic sense," writes Daniel Costello in the *Wall Street Journal.* "By tailoring the homes to boomers' tastes—with everything from marble floors to Surround Sound stereo systems, to his-and-hers bathrooms—[developers] bet they could reel in middle-managers and expand their market."

Costello continues, "The middle-aged crowd, in turn, is signing up in droves, both to take advantage of the lifestyle luxuries and to lock up a place to retire before real estate prices rise beyond their means."

There does appear to be one slight negative to promoting senior living communities to the baby boomers: Some sixty-five-and-up seniors may get a little irritated by all the activity of the younger baby boomers. But this attitude is by no means held by all seniors. Norma Rache, age sixty-eight, a resident of Tellico Village in Loudown, Tennessee, says the mixture of seniors and boomers makes the community seem like one big extended family. For her, "The younger people add spice and energy."[6]

Where to Live?

Where you want to live depends upon your priorities. Do you want to be with other seniors? Florida has the highest percent of population age sixty-five and over. Alaska has the lowest. This comes as no surprise. On the other hand, Alaska has no state income tax, no sales tax, and seniors over sixty-five are exempt from property tax. The state of New York has the highest of these three taxes combined. The most affordable housing can be found at Lake Martin, Alabama. The least affordable housing is at Carmel, California. Of course, the fact that Carmel has the best climate may have something to do with housing costs. Looking for work? Then San Diego is the place to go. Western Colorado has the worst chances for work. The highest cost of living is in Laguna Beach, California (near Los Angeles). The lowest cost of living, on the other hand, is in the Bitterroot Valley of Montana. Look, you can't have everything. The lowest doctor-to-patient ratio is in Nevada; the highest in Washington, D.C. The fastest growing population is in western Arizona. The highest nursing home occupancy is in Mississippi; the lowest in Texas. And for golfers, it will come as no surprise that Hilton Head, South Carolina, has the most public golf holes per person.[7]

At Luther Crest we are seeing people who retired to Florida coming back north. We understand it is occurring in other home-state retirement communities as well, and there are several reasons.

Crowding has become unbearable for some seniors. Not only are there many retirees in the state, but winter vacationers and year-round tourists to Orlando and similar vacation destinations have crowded the roads, restaurants, golf courses, and other public facilities. "It's too much of a hassle" commented one of our Luther Crest residents who had been in Florida for a decade.

Distance from family also motivates seniors to move north, or never choose to move to Florida in the first place. As people age and need assistance in daily functions, family members are frequently called upon to provide help or arrange for it. When nursing care is needed, family involvement in insuring good care becomes crucial. The separation of seniors from their families can put a great strain on all involved. A study published in 1997 by the National Council on Aging and the Pew Charitable Trust found that almost 80 percent of long-distance caregivers experience some negative effects as a result of their efforts, including damage to their own health, high levels of stress, and interference with their personal lives.[8]

Bill and Ginny moved to a gated senior community outside Savannah about ten years ago. In their Christmas card they wrote, "The year 2000 was good to us and finds us still enjoying Savannah even though many of our friends have made changes this year to be nearer their families or to seek health care."

Apart from health reasons, though, seniors want to be closer to their grandchildren. The dream of having grandchildren come to visit their grandparents in Arizona or Florida does not often come to pass more than once a year. So, the grandparents move back to where they can enjoy their grandchildren more often.

The lack of cultural opportunities is cited by some people as reason for not wanting to move south. While Miami and Phoenix are not without good music and art, they are nowhere near the symphonies of New York, Boston, Philadelphia, Cleveland, and Chicago, the opera and theater of New York, and the magnificent museums of the Northeast and Upper Midwest.

Then there is the importance of friends. Friends of ours who have moved to Florida say it is easy to develop new friendships. I believe them because most of the people in the places where seniors buy are in the same boat. They have come from the north and many of them want to establish new friendships.

But the matter of friendship is subjective. Some of us are loners and really are happy not relating to many others. Others of us are content to have a handful of good friends with whom we interact. Still others enjoy having large numbers of friends. Judith and I are in this last category. As we moved around the country, we always entertained large groups, became deeply involved in the life of whatever church we joined, and volunteered to work in community organizations. For us, the thought of moving away in our senior years never entered our minds.

Finally, for Christians who wish to give back to society through various kinds of ministry, location is important. While ministry in senior living can be carried out anywhere, the fact that many of us already have ministries in our community should be an important factor to consider if we are thinking about moving elsewhere. Others who are just entering the postretirement years have a well-established local network that will lead them into new ministries.

For Judith and me, the place for our senior living was a nobrainer. We want to be fairly close to our family, we enjoy the proximity to New York and the cultural opportunities that surround us, we greatly cherish our many friends here, and we already have ministries in our community and our church.

Where to live and when to make changes in living locations is certainly one of the most important parts of planning for senior living. It is not at all unreasonable for people in their thirties to draw up a long-range plan for this aspect of senior living. And, like any long-range plans, there should be a time line.

To paraphrase Martin Trueblood, the people who make the best transitions in senior living are those who take action before they must.

chapter
five
lifestyle

Judith and I have attended almost all our high school reunions, held every five years. Since we graduated from high school two years apart, it means that in any five-year period we attend two reunions. A remarkable change has occurred since the earliest reunions.

In the fifth- and tenth-year reunions, everyone was still sharing their experiences from the Second World War, the colleges from which they graduated, and the babies they had. It was clear who among us had advanced up the military ranks and who were combat soldiers. There was a clear divide between those of us who went on to college and those of us who did not. There was even a divide between those of us who attended the big-name universities and those of us who went to small teachers' colleges. None of us were wealthy, but we all dressed up as best we could for the big reunion dance. The "big men in high school," namely the athletes, were still the "big men" at the reunion. The cheerleaders generally were still the best-looking women; however, we all were about on an equal footing when it came to comparing baby pictures of our children.

By the fifteenth- and twentieth-year reunions, wealth and prestigious jobs began to show. Some of the women were dressed elegantly and the men wore the latest in fashion. There was a great interest in "What are you doing now?" The high school heroes were not quite the "big men" they used to be, although they thought so.

By the twenty-fifth reunion it became apparent which of us were "making it" in life. Some of us had pictures to show of our children standing in front of large homes, some arrived in expensive cars, some had become judges, and one was a governor. Lee Iacocca, a member of my class, was so famous he stopped coming to mere high school reunions. Attendance began to drop, not because of death or illness, but because people felt they did not measure up to the so-called success criteria that we were, at least implicitly, applying to ourselves. They stopped coming because they had not gained the material and social successes that were being used as measurements, or because they had no stories of exotic places they had visited, or tales of the prestigious universities their children were attending.

By the fiftieth reunion, everything was different. We were in our late sixties and our values had changed considerably. Titles and social position went virtually unnoticed. Wealth was totally ignored. What was important was the sharing of school memories, even going back to elementary school. (I later hosted a reunion party of my second-grade class—about a dozen of us could be identified and lived nearby.) There were few of the athletic heroes around—many had dropped out over the years as their fame had faded. Also, only a small group of the noncollege people was present.

As I look back on it all, it was sad that so many people stopped coming over the years because they did not measure up to our values of materialism and social standing. I have discussed this evolution of high school reunions with friends from other areas and find similar experiences.

"At your twenty-fifth high school reunion, you'd better be successful—or at least good looking. At your fiftieth, no one cares," writes Dan Wakefield in his article on high school class reunions.[1] Quite possibly, it is because we are seeing more of our classmates die that we have chucked our interest in the superficial things of life. Now we are more focused on friend-ships and memories. We have simplified our values. Our lifestyle has changed significantly.

Let it be said that not all seniors are experiencing the liber-ating sense of simplicity that has overtaken our high school reunions. Some people are still focused on wealth. One couple we know from our church, in their early sixties, is building their "dream home." It is huge. Four bedrooms, four and one-half baths, a spacious kitchen, all the latest in security gadgetry, a large den, a large office, a three-car garage, a swimming pool, and spacious gardens. I innocently asked why they are going so large scale with no children at home. "We earned it!" was the reply. "Our kids are all through college, and we both will be retiring soon. We want a large place where we can entertain friends and accommodate our children and future grand-children when they come to visit." I carefully got to the issue of a three-car garage for only two cars. "Oh, that's for resale. When we do have to sell the place, we want it to be fully up-to-date." Makes sense, I guess.

Another couple we know owns a condo in the Bahamas. They divide their year between their attractive home in our area and the sandy beaches of their island condo. "We don't play golf much anymore, but we love to relax on the beach, soak up the sun, and eat at some great restaurants," she said. "This is real living."

Why is it that some of us have become more relaxed about life while others of us are still caught in the frenzy of amassing and consuming material wealth? Some cannot let go of a life of clutter and confusion. They seem to be denying their senior years. By continuing a life of acquiring more stuff, of trying to outdo their cohorts and by appearing young and vigorous, are they refusing to think about advancing age? And does this lifestyle make them happy?

Qualities of a Mature Senior Life

Many researchers and observers of the aging process have developed lists of qualities for a positive, mature senior life. I have culled through their lists and submit what might be a consensus report on the signs of an ideal senior lifestyle. They are not listed in any particular order.

1. Maturing seniors have the courage and ability to change. While some seniors resist all forms of change, the positive senior is able to negotiate changes in life and has the courage to try new ideas. We see this daily among the seniors at Luther Crest. Those seniors who are reluctant to change tend to be crabby complainers. Nothing ever seems to be right. On the other hand, those who are open to new ideas and new ways are invariably happier and friendlier people.

2. Mature seniors enjoy other people. They easily make new friends. They get along in any type of group. Seldom will you hear them make a negative or unkind remark about anyone.

3. Mature seniors are independent. They are able to do their own thing and pay their own way. They are also independent thinkers who do not give in to pressure to accept society's norms.

4. Mature seniors are positive and hopeful about the future, despite the fact that they are aging. They bear their physical frailties with hope and good humor.

5. Mature seniors have a sound spirituality. They trust God and can speak freely about their faith. They maintain membership in a church or other religious organization. They continue to see purpose in their lives. They pray regularly, giving thanks for what God has given them today, asking for healing for their friends and blessings for the individual members of their families.

6. Mature seniors continue to learn and have an active mind. They keep up-to-date on world events. You will meet them at senior citizen centers, in local college programs for seniors, and at Elderhostels all over the world. They love art, music, drama, and travel.

7. Mature seniors are very active volunteers.

8. Mature seniors are generous with their financial assets.

9. Mature seniors with an ideal lifestyle care for other people, for their environment, and for society. They visit those who are sick, recycle their goods wherever possible, and help in social causes.

10. Mature seniors care for their own bodies. They watch their diet carefully and exercise regularly, often keeping restrictions on smoking and alcohol consumption. They get periodic physical checkups and follow their physician's advice.

11. Mature seniors tend to simplify their lives. Material goods and peer-group pressure to buy more than they need are of no concern to them.

12. Mature seniors freely express their emotions. Laughter, tears, and a big hug come naturally.

13. Mature seniors are generally happy and content with life. Disappointment, aches, and losses do not defeat them. They always bounce back.

More qualities of mature seniors could be added, but many of the examples listed above were consistent themes in the research. Must a senior have all the above traits in order to be considered a mature person? Certainly not. The list simply represents the traits most frequently observed in seniors having a positive lifestyle.

Much to my surprise, none of the lists of traits for a positive senior lifestyle mentioned one trait that I think is important: thankfulness. I want to include it as number fourteen on the list.

Thankfulness

I am thankful to God for all the blessings I have received throughout my lifetime. I am thankful for a courageous mother who kept on going after my father left us in the midst of the Great Depression, for friends and family who helped us. I am thankful for teachers who encouraged me to do better and for a college that awarded me a scholarship when we had no money for me to continue my education. This may seem strange, but I am also thankful that I experienced the horror of combat in

World War II and, of course, thankful I survived. I am thankful that Judith and I came together. I am thankful for my experiences as a young steel salesman in Detroit. I am thankful for four children, nine grandchildren, two sons-in-law, and a daughter-in-law. I am thankful for the way my faith has grown in the churches we attended and the wonderful friends who came into our lives. I am thankful for the fine management jobs I had at Bethlehem Steel and for the opportunity to retire early to do community work. And I am especially thankful that God answered our impassioned prayers the night our son Billy almost died, and for faith in those terrifying hours when Judith was so sick she did not care to live anymore. The list could go on, but think about it yourself. Reflect on your life and count the blessings for which you can give thanks.

The Scriptures, especially in the Psalms, talk of giving thanks. "Offer to God a sacrifice of thanksgiving" (Ps. 50:14). "Let us come into his presence with thanksgiving" (Ps. 95:2). "Give thanks to the Lord, for he is good; his steadfast love endures forever" (Ps. 118:1). "Sing to the Lord with thanksgiving" (Ps. 147:7).

When Jesus fed the multitude, "he took the seven loaves, and after giving thanks he broke them and gave them to his disciples to distribute" (Mark 8:6). At the Last Supper, Jesus "took a cup, and after giving thanks he gave it to them" (Matt. 26:27; see also Luke 22:17).

The apostle Paul frequently gives thanks when writing to the young churches: "First, I thank my God through Jesus Christ for all of you" (Rom. 1:8). "I give thanks to my God always for you" (1 Cor. 1:4).

My favorite prayer of thankfulness for God is Psalm 103. Our family has always used the first lines as our thanksgiving before meals: "Bless the Lord, O my soul, and all that is within me, bless his holy name. Bless the Lord, O my soul, and do not forget all his benefits." The psalm enumerates all the things for which we give God thanks: "who forgives all your iniquity, who heals all your diseases" (v. 3); "who satisfies you with good" (v. 5); "The Lord is merciful and gracious, slow to anger and abounding in steadfast love" (v. 8); "He does not deal with us according to our sins, nor repay us according to our iniquities" (v. 10); "As a father has compassion for his children, so the Lord has compassion for those who fear him" (v. 13); "But the steadfast love of the Lord is from everlasting to everlasting on those who fear him, and his righteousness to children's children" (v. 17). Most certainly, the mature senior is one who is thankful and shows it.

Be Not Afraid

The fourth quality listed of mature seniors is that they are positive and hopeful for the future. This book is being written on the heels of the worst terrorist strikes ever to hit our nation. We are in a war to abolish terrorism. How long that will take we do not know. With the memory of the attacks of September 11, 2001, many Americans live in fear of more terrorist attacks. Major airlines were on the verge of bankruptcy for lack of passengers, and in August 2002, U.S. Airways did file for protection under Chapter 11. Restaurants, theaters, and music halls experienced decreased attendance as people ate at home and watched television. Our infrastructure of airports, government buildings, bridges, tunnels, water systems, and nuclear power plants were heavily protected by our military reserves. Anthrax sent a scare throughout the East Coast. We were warned that terrorist groups have access to nuclear and biological instruments of mass destruction.

In the face of all this, are mature seniors remaining positive and hopeful? Well, to a great extent, yes. We are not positive that terrorism will soon be ended. Nor are we positive that there will not be more terrorist acts, perhaps more dreadful than the destruction of the World Trade Center in New York. Nor do we anticipate that this new kind of war will end soon.

But in general, seniors are not afraid—at least not the seniors we know. There are several obvious reasons for this: We no longer have responsibilities for our immediate families or our jobs. We have tried to live our lives well and know that we will encounter death anyway somewhere down the road. Beyond those obvious reasons, as Christians we remember many Bible admonitions not to be afraid.

My unabridged Bible concordance lists an astonishing number of places where the words *fear* and *afraid* appear. Fear, as a verb, appears sixty-four times; "fear of the Lord," thirty-four times; and "fear God," eleven times. Similarly, the word *afraid* appears fifty-two times; "be afraid," eleven times; and "sore afraid," ten times. In short, the Bible bears witness to the fact that fear is a common human emotion.

But the concordance also lists "do not fear" sixty times; "fear not," sixty-five times; "be not afraid," fourteen times; and "not be afraid," twelve times. It is God or God's angels who most frequently speak the admonition to not be afraid or fear not. "Do not be afraid, Abram, I am your shield; your reward shall be very great" (Gen. 15:1). "And the Lord said to Joshua, 'Do not be afraid of them' " (Josh. 11:6). "You will not fear the terror of the night, or the arrow that flies by day, or the pestilence that stalks in darkness, or the destruction that wastes at noonday" (Ps. 91:5-6). "Do not be afraid of sudden panic, or of the storm that strikes the wicked; for the Lord will be your confidence and will keep your foot from being caught" (Prov. 3:25-26). "Do not fear those who kill the body but cannot kill the soul" (Matt. 10:28). "But immediately Jesus spoke to them and said 'Take heart, it is I; do not be afraid' " (Matt. 14:27; see also Mark 6:50 and John 6:20). "Do not be afraid, I am the first and the last, and the living one" (Rev. 1:17-18).

This is a time, it seems to [me,] that Christians who are seniors can play an important role by reminding our brothers and sisters that God is with us. We will not fear; however, we know there is great danger out there. But we have been through dangerous times before. We will face these days with hope and will not be afraid. That is another ministry for seniors.

Learning

There are numerous opportunities for seniors to learn. Our local senior citizen center has a wide range of courses in computers, arts and crafts, ballroom and line dancing, history, foreign languages, and many other subjects. You have to get your reservations in early because of high demand.

At Luther Crest we have a computer room where skilled volunteers teach computer literacy and help more advanced people with computer problems. All seniors should be computer literate; after all, our young grandchildren are!

A local college is the home for a "Learning in Retirement" program. Short courses consisting of four to six weekly sessions are offered on all kinds of topics and taught by former professors or other experts in their fields.

Our congregation has a seniors group with an active and diverse program. One subgroup, known as Intellectual Stimulation, has a program every other week on all kinds of topics, both religious and secular.

Let's admit it: we have a literacy problem with our Bible. Senior living is an ideal time to correct this deficiency. In our church, a former theology professor offers a Bible-reading program every Monday evening. It is well attended and continues on by popular demand.

Some of the best learning experiences Judith and I have shared are the Elderhostels. Since we were married, we have traveled to twenty-two foreign countries. Sometimes it was with a commercial tour; sometimes we went alone or with another couple. But we vote Elderhostels as the most educational trips we have taken. There are several reasons. First, and foremost, the Elderhostel trips we have taken were designed and presented by a university in the area. Thus we have excellent lectures presented by fine teachers. A second benefit is the type of people who attend. Not only do they move at about the same speed we do, but they are all interesting people and are eager to learn. Generally, you stay in one place. None of this "Bags packed and in the hallway by 6:00 A. M.!," which is often typical of commercial tour groups.

For example, our trip to western Ireland placed us in a hotel in Ennis with day trips to various parts of the country. Same thing with Elderhostels in Savannah, Georgia; Charleston, South Carolina; and in Nogales, Arizona. On our trip down the Mississippi River from Nashville to New Orleans, our nights were all spent on the boat. That trip, called "Music of the Mississippi," was one of our best Elderhostels, with excellent lectures and many musical groups coming on board to show us how music along the Mississippi River changes from town to town.

Finally, Elderhostel costs are bargains. The hotels have always been good, as has been the food. Don't expect the Waldorf Astoria and pheasant under glass. But then neither will you have to put up with typical Waldorf prices.

Materialism

Being materialistic is not on my earlier list of thirteen senior lifestyles that make for well-balanced senior living. It is instead listed as an opposite to simple living, which is number eleven on the list. But because materialism and its partner, consumerism, are so ingrained in American culture, it is difficult to put them aside as one goes into senior living. They are addictive. This chapter cannot deal with senior lifestyle without confronting materialism face to face.

Materialism is a worldview that defines physical well-being and worldly possessions as constituting the greatest good and highest value in life. This worldview, which is almost a "doctrine" for some, is what drives some seniors to pursue a life of total self-indulgence. It is a life of elegant condominium living, of playing golf or tennis or fishing or sailing every day, of sunning on Caribbean islands, of wearing the latest high fashions, of eating and drinking at expensive restaurants, of driving costly sports cars, and of not giving a thought about the rest of the world. Some seniors truly covet such a lifestyle.

The prophet Amos had some harsh words for those whose lives are given over to self-indulgence:

Alas for those who lie on beds of ivory,
    and lounge on their couches,
and eat lambs from the flock,
    and calves from the stall,
who sing idle songs to the sound of the harp,
    and like David improvise on instruments of music;
who drink wine from bowls
    and anoint themselves with the finest oils,
    but are not grieved over the ruin of Joseph! (Amos 6:4-6)

Jesus used many material things to illustrate his sayings and parables, including the lost coin, loaves and fish, the mustard seed, a candle on a stand, and a lost sheep. Material things are neutral, neither good nor bad in themselves. But it is the amassing of material goods and the lust for them that is evil. Jesus is very direct in his assertion that "you cannot serve God and wealth" (Matt. 6:24; some Bible translations use the Greek word for wealth, *mammon*).

Robert Wuthnow, in his book *God and Mammon in America*, suggests that most Americans feel they can serve God and mammon without compromising their religious beliefs. Wuthnow's basic premise is that most Christians differentiate between the spiritual and the material. The spiritual side of one's life has little or no connection to the physical or material; for example, "when working Americans are asked directly about the role of religion in their job choices, most say that their decision was not influenced by religion."[2] What was a major influence behind choice of occupation? You guessed it: "the money."

At least half of the people responding to a survey about personal materialism answered that the following material items or activities were either fairly important, very important, or absolutely essential.

Having a high paying job	80 percent
Having a beautiful home, a new car, and other nice things	78 percent
Wearing nice clothes	75 percent
Being able to travel for pleasure and see interesting things	72 percent
Eating out at nice restaurants	50 percent[3]

Wuthnow concluded that committed churchgoers were just as materialistic as the nonreligious; on the other hand, most of the churchgoing people Wuthnow surveyed felt that materialism was an important social problem (83 percent) and too much emphasis has been placed on money (84 percent).[4]

While churchgoing people are no less materialistic in their actions, "three persons in four say they would like churches and synagogues to encourage people to be less materialistic."[5] When was the last time your pastor preached against materialism or excessive consumerism?

To summarize Wuthnow's work on the topic of God and mammon in America, churchgoing people are no less materialistic than society as a whole, they tend to see no connection between faith and economics, yet they sense materialism is wrong and wish the churches would preach more against it. How's that for contradiction? Yet I think he is absolutely right.

Anthony O'Hear, taking a secular approach to the affluence and stability of our nation, charges us not to blind ourselves to the discontent of those who have "made it." He reminds us that progress in one area of life is usually accompanied by losses in other areas.[6]

One day while I was teaching my class on religion, ethics, and business at Muhlenberg College, I made one of my frequent disparaging comments on the greed of a certain prominent Wall Street trader.

One of the students raised his hand and asked, "Mr. Diehl, what's wrong with greed?" The question stopped me for a moment because I naively assumed that everyone felt that greed was a negative attribute. I asked him if he had a dictionary on his computer and he answered yes. I asked him to look up the word *greed* and read the meaning to all of us. In a moment he read out loud, "Greed, noun, a rapacious desire for more than one needs or deserves, as of food, wealth, or power." Then he said, "So?"

"So a greedy person *always* wants more. A greedy person is never satisfied. A greedy person will go through life feeling unfulfilled amidst riches far more than one can imagine," I responded.

"I think that would be an exciting way to live!" the student replied.

I guess he did not get the point, or perhaps he did. From time to time, I tell others about the student who asked, "What's wrong with greed?" I then ask them how they would answer the question. Some say that greed is a sin according to the Bible. Others simply say that it is up to the individual.

John D. Rockefeller was once asked how much money it would take to be really satisfied. He answered, "Just a little bit more."[7] No contentment can come into a life that forever is needing "a little bit more" of money or prestige or authority or security.

So why is it that some seniors get to a point in life where no one cares anymore about material possessions, while other seniors seem to be obsessed with the continued accumulation of material goods?

The problem may be that some of us are not aware of the forces at work in our society that seek to dominate our lives. The New Testament refers to these societal forces as "principalities and powers." In his letter to the church at Rome, Paul writes, "For I am convinced that neither death, nor life, nor angels, nor *principalities*, nor things present, nor things to come, nor *powers*, nor height, nor depth, nor anything else in all creation, will be able to separate us from the love of God in Christ Jesus our Lord" (Rom. 8:38, RSV, emphasis mine).

Again, in his letter to the Ephesians, Paul refers to the powers when he writes, "For we are not contending against flesh and blood, but the *principalities*, against the *powers*, against the world rulers of this present darkness, against the spiritual hosts of wickedness in the heavenly places" (Ephesians 6:12, RSV, emphasis mine).

In Colossians 1:16, Paul states that since God is the creator of all things, the powers are also of his creation. The powers, however, have become among the spiritual forces of evil in society. How do we define the powers today?

Theologian John Howard Yoder lists intellectual structures— "the 'ologies' and 'isms'"—among the powers that "have absolutized themselves and demand from the individual and society an unconditional loyalty. They harm and enslave man."[8]

Think about the "isms" of today: totalitarianism, socialism, communism, consumerism, alcoholism, humanism, egalitarianism, capitalism, asceticism, narcissism, materialism, and many more. The "isms" take over our lives and demand our complete support of them, almost to the exclusion of all other interests. They dominate us. They are demonic.

Materialism can put us in an endless cycle of work-spend-work-spend that goes well beyond our basic needs. For example, Jesse, age thirty-nine, was making good money as a technician at Agere's Optoelectronics Center near Allentown. "He and his wife decided to lease their 'dream car,' a $38,000 Toyota 4Runner Limited Edition, with leather interior and compact disc player," writes reporter Christian Berg. "They took vacations, remodeled the kitchen and living room and had central air conditioning installed."

Berg continues, "Last fall, Agere could hardly keep up with demand for its fiber-optic products. That meant overtime was plentiful. Jesse grabbed as much of it as he could. It was nothing to work ten and twelve hours a day."

"The more I made, the more we spent," Jesse said. "We'd buy clothes, and go out to eat a lot. If you take all the kids, you could drop $100 just to go to eat. And it was no problem because all I had to do was work every day."[9]

Our passion to possess is fueled daily by a powerful economic system built largely upon consumerism. Think about it. Television has come to be 50 percent program and 50 percent commercials urging us to buy something. Not just anything, but something better than what we now have. Consider all the automobile commercials. The sponsors know we all have cars already, but they want us to buy newer, better, more expensive cars. The last thing a producer or salesman wants is for you to be satisfied, for then you will stop buying. Advertising is used to convince you that you need something more. At least half of your local newspaper is advertising. Coupons abound to get you into a particular store. At least half of most magazines' content consists of advertising. Roadside billboards advertise. Trains, buses, sports arenas—wherever you look there is advertising.

Advertising is particularly ferocious because companies with competing products want you to buy their brand. Don't buy any toothpaste, buy Crest—at least one of the ten different types of Crest you will find on your supermarket's shelves. Don't buy any kind of sports shoes, buy Nike.

The pressure to buy the "in" thing is especially successful with children. And it can be tragic. Imagine the pressure put on a parent living in poverty when a child insists he must have expensive Nike sports shoes in order to fit in with a group that bases its acceptance of other kids on what they wear. Parents may skimp on food or let other bills go unpaid rather than have their child ostracized by his peer group. Chalk up another victory for consumerism!

I have always resented the way the fashion industry manipulates what we wear. Wide lapels, narrow lapels, wide ties, narrow ties, and on and on (not to mention the manipulation of women's fashions!). Yet, I must confess that in my days at Bethlehem Steel, I went along with the trends just so I would fit in.

Consumerism is so important to our country that it is a major economic barometer. Consumer confidence is considered one of the primary precursors of which way our national economy is going. Is it any wonder that so many Americans are addicted to material goods, and not just *any* material goods, but the latest material goods?

Make no mistake about it: Materialism is a spiritual issue. So is consumerism. To the extent that we seek security in the amassing of material goods we, in effect, worship another god. "Because the plausibility of consumerism depends entirely on the apparent permanence of life in this world," writes Craig M. Gay, "we must continually remind each other—and ourselves— that this world and its lusts are indeed passing away."[10]

Do seniors want to live out the rest of their lives under the demonic power of materialism? And what can people do who are addicted to consumerism and materialism? The same thing they do when they are addicted to tobacco or alcohol or drugs. They must first want to change.

A materialistic addict must recite the mantra, "You cannot serve God and wealth" until it becomes part of his or her life. Here's a scary story for a wealth addict:

> A certain ruler once asked Jesus what he must do to inherit eternal life. Jesus said, "You know the commandments: you shall not commit adultery; you shall not murder; you shall not steal; you shall not bear false witness; honor your father and mother." The ruler said, "I have kept all these since my youth." When Jesus heard this he said to him, "There is still one thing lacking. Sell all that you own and distribute the money to the poor, and you will have treasure in heaven; then come, follow me." But when he heard this, he became sad; for he was very rich. Jesus looked at him and said, "How hard it is for those who have wealth to enter the kingdom of God! Indeed it is easier for a camel to go through the eye of a needle than for someone who is rich to enter the kingdom of God."
>
> Those who heard it said, "Then who can be saved?" Jesus replied, "What is impossible for mortals is possible for God." (Luke 18:20-27; see also Matt. 19:16-26 and Mark 10:17-27)

I have read various interpretations of the "eye of the needle" story but the real focus should be on "What is impossible for mortals is possible for God." Mortals, by virtue of their wealth, cannot enter the kingdom of God. But it is by the grace of God that one enters the kingdom. The grace of God will accept a person of wealth into the kingdom provided that person serves God and not wealth. And only God knows. As seniors, we are free to reject the demons of materialism and consumerism.

An advantage of living in a retirement community is that materialistic peer pressure is virtually gone. We all live in essentially the same level of housing—no big homes and little homes. We all eat at the same "restaurant," attend the same parties, travel to the symphony or theater on the same bus, and receive the same housekeeping and groundskeeping services. With respect to clothing, people wear about the same clothes as they did before coming to the retirement community. The style of men's clothing says more about their age than about their wealth. We buy new clothes only when we wear out the older ones. Fashion changes have no control over us. The women's clothes tend to speak more of the preretirement days of wealth than of their existing conditions; that is, some women have elegant and obviously expensive clothes but they, too, are not obviously recently purchased.

With respect to former positions in business and community, it is impossible to tell until you get to know someone very well. Men do not sport "CEO" or "Judge" or "College President" buttons on their jackets. The only exceptions are the medical doctors and clergy doctors who prefer to be called "Doctor" by the staff.

In short, a retirement community can free people from whatever material pressures they once had. Living in a continuing care-retirement community is one of the ways that senior living enables us to move into a life of simplicity.

Simplicity

There is an old Shaker hymn that goes:

'Tis a gift to be simple,
'Tis a gift to be free,
'Tis a gift to come down where we ought to be,
And when we see ourselves in a way that's right,
We will live in a valley of love and delight.
When true simplicity is gained
To live and to love we will not be ashamed,
To turn and to turn will be our delight,
Till by turning, turning
We turn 'round right.

Richard Foster writes that for Christians, "Simplicity is an *inward* reality that results in an outward lifestyle."[11] He also says:

Christian simplicity is not just a faddish attempt to respond to the ecological holocaust that threatens to engulf us, nor is it born out of frustration with technocratic obesity. It is a call to every Christian. The witness to simplicity is profoundly rooted in the biblical tradition, and most perfectly exemplified in the life of Jesus Christ. In one form or another, all the devotional masters have stressed its essential nature. It is a natural and necessary outflow of the Good News of the Gospel having taken root in our lives.[12]

A Theology of Enough

Exodus tells the story of how God provided manna for the Israelites as they wandered in the wilderness. God told Moses that enough manna would be provided each day for each person. "They gathered as much as each of them needed." They were instructed to take no more than they needed. Moses said, "Let no one leave any of it over until morning." "But they did not listen to Moses; some left part of it until morning, and it bred worms and became foul" (see Exod. 16-18). It is a wonderful story of what happens when people do not trust God and take for themselves more than enough for the day.

The story is the basis of a delightful book, *Enough Is Enough*, by John V. Taylor.[13] God has provided so much for us, really more than we need. Taylor's chapter on "A Theology of Enough" suggests that we keep for ourselves only as much as we really need; the rest belongs to someone who does not have enough to meet his or her needs.

While I have not had the courage to practice Taylor's suggestion literally, it has been a helpful concept in my purchase of material goods. I have tried to make the purchase of a car or clothing or a house on the basis of what was necessary to take care of my family and do my job. I did not need the latest and the greatest of material goods to care for my family or carry out my job as a sales manager. But I did require that those things be "good enough."

And how do we seniors decide what is "enough"? As we downsize our housing, how many rooms do we really need? How many bedrooms, baths, and other rooms does a couple need? Many years ago we bought a year-round vacation home in the mountains. Do we really need it? Probably not, but if we didn't have it we would be spending money on renting vacation facilities each year. (See how easy it is to rationalize?)

Does a senior family need more than one car? We still have two. The older, larger Mercury is used on long trips to visit family. Judith's newer, smaller Toyota is used to get her around town to her many volunteer activities. But both cars are in use perhaps only 20 percent of the time. When we consider going to one car, I insist on a larger one because I am so tall. Judith insists on a smaller one to get around town. So do we really need two cars?

Judith likes to keep up with changes in clothing fashion. I want to wear my suits, sport coats, ties, and shoes until they wear out. Do I look like an old geezer when we go out? Yup, but I don't care—most of the time.

When we travel somewhere by auto we always stay at the bottom-of-the-line motels. "As long as it's clean" is Judith's only requirement. It's a little more difficult when we travel overseas. The lowest-priced travel package may be a dog. That's one reason why we will book with Elderhostel if a program is available when and where we plan to go. The theology of enough sounds simple, but when we try to carry it out, it becomes complex.

Foster warns that Christian simplicity does not lead to simplistic answers to complex problems. We still have to contend with the "principalities and powers" that the apostle Paul refers to.

Christian simplicity is based on the conviction that we are loved and accepted by God; not because of our good deeds, but because of God's grace which we are free to accept. Knowing and believing that, we work on complex issues as best we can with the teachings of Jesus kept firmly in mind. That is not to say that his words can always be applied literally to today's complex problems. But it is the spirit of his teachings that shall guide our decision-making. Using that spirit and the brains the good Lord has given us, we approach complex problems and "sin boldly," as Martin Luther said. That is, with the knowledge that we are imperfect individuals, we make decisions allowing for the possibility that we may be wrong.

Active Caring

The ninth trait that we listed for mature seniors was "They care—for other people, for their environment, and for their society." That says to me that mature seniors are always concerned with issues of the day. Senior living does not mean that we live as if on some distant planet, far removed from the cares of our world. No, seniors continue to read, discuss, and, at times, take action.

Seniors are in an especially good position to be advocates for people and issues. Advocacy is an action method of caring for people, the environment, and society. "Remember, concentrate on the super voters!" Those were the primary words of instruction I got the first time I participated in a phone-a-thon on behalf of a friend of mine who was running for political office. About eight of us were gathered at the office of a real estate company whose owner was a supporter of the candidate. It was after business hours and he had turned over all his phones for us to use.

The campaign manager gave each of us about ten sheets listing the names, addresses, phone numbers, and dates each person had voted in the past four years. The records are public information and can be obtained from the county simply for the cost of reproducing them. Those persons with four or more stars behind their names (six was the maximum possible) were considered "super voters"—those most likely to vote in the next election.

And who were these super voters? Largely seniors—those over age fifty-five. It did not matter what their political party affiliation was, Republican, Democratic, or Independent—the seniors were much more likely to vote than all other eligible voters.

A study made at Case Western University showed that although the percentage of "sixty-five plus" eligible voters was fairly constant from 1968 to 1996, the percentage of "sixty-five plus" voters who cast ballots increased from less than 16 percent of all votes in 1968 to slightly over 20 percent of all votes cast in 1996.

Much has been said about the steady falling participation of eligible voters in elections over the past twenty-five years, but not among the "sixty-five plus" group. Their level of participation has remained steady.[14] So important is the senior vote that many politicians carefully steer clear of tampering with Social Security and Medicare benefits unless there is an effort to enhance them.

Yet the perception that all seniors tend to vote the same way on public issues is just that—a perception. "Older Americans, in their behavior and beliefs, are probably more diverse than any younger group," says Debra Street, a research fellow at the Pepper Institute on Aging and Public Policy at Florida State University.[15]

In 2000, there were 34.7 million people over age sixty-five (I cannot find a comparable number for people over fifty-five). By

2010, the number will be 39.4 million and by 2020, it will be 53.2 million. If seniors maintain their high level of voter participation, they will become an increasingly important influence in our country. Notice the "if" in that sentence. Recent studies have shown that young voters (age eighteen to twenty-four) are voting at lower rates than their age group did in 1972. Because of cynicism in regard to national politics, younger people are turning away from voting for national, state, and local candidates.

"At a time when the nation as a whole is tuning out public debate and tuning into neighborhood and community service, Generation Xers are leading both trends," writes Elizabeth Crowley.[16] Of course, today's community volunteer can become tomorrow's super voter. Whatever way the numbers develop, political involvement should be an important part of the lifestyle of seniors. And it's not just voting. Actively support candidates. Volunteer to help a local person running for office. You will not be turned down. Your commitment may be for just a few months, but it is fun and exciting. Also, consider submitting your name for locally appointed spots on boards or commissions. The positions are not compensated, but you learn a lot and do provide a service.

I am on the Lehigh County Housing Authority, appointed by our county executive. Of the five persons on our authority, two are retired seniors, one is a working senior, and two are younger working people.

Better still, why not run for a local office? Seniors with good life experience and plenty of time to give to the office are attractive candidates. Winning an election and serving in a local office—school board, town council, town mayor—is particularly gratifying for a woman, as Judith found out for herself. She will be heard and taken seriously. She will serve as a role model for other women. She will be able to advance her own agenda. Most important, the "just a woman" stereotype will be shattered.

Furthermore, we all can express our feelings on public issues through letters to the editor in our newspaper. I recall the day I was flying to Washington, D.C., on a morning plane. We were all seated and the doors were about to close when our U.S. representative ducked into the plane and sat down in the row in front of me. Out of his briefcase he took the local morning paper. Without even looking at the first page, he turned directly to the editorial page and read all the letters to the editor. That told me something about the importance of letters to the editor.

Writing letters to your newspaper or public officials can continue well into old age. It is a way that people who are homebound can actively participate in the political process. I write letters to our local paper but have to be choosy about my issues because there is a limit on how frequently the same person can get his or her letter printed. But writing letters is an easy thing to do. Try it.

Writing letters directly to your local leaders or state and national representatives is more effective than one would think. A friend of mine who is now in the state senate of Pennsylvania says that he counts one personal letter on an issue as ten. Not so for the preprinted letter that some interest group wants us to sign. They count only as one, he says, and sometimes less. But personal letters, even handwritten, count as ten since he feels that if one person took the time to write him on some issue, there are probably nine more who feel the same way.

As President George W. Bush was trying to get his major tax-cut bill through Congress in early 2001, all kinds of groups were trying to influence the outcome. The U.S. Chamber of Commerce and other lobbies were trying to support the major cut for high-income persons. Some groups were trying to eliminate the so-called marriage tax, others wanted to kill the death tax. That's the way it is in Washington. There are lobbyists for and against environmental legislation, education, the military, foreign relations, and so forth.

But there is one group that has no lobbyists, no organized interest group. It's poor people. Except for some suggestions of a few concerned senators, the poor were given very little consideration and no voice in the drafting of President Bush's major piece of tax legislation.

The tragedy of all this is that it is the *children* of the poor who are the innocent victims of poverty. Almost 20 percent of the children of our nation live in poverty. Through no fault of their own, they receive less nutrition, go to poorer schools, live in more dangerous neighborhoods, and inhabit sub-standard housing. It is not surprising that these children are more likely than their cohorts to need medical attention.

And, of course, there are seniors living in poverty also. Paul Recer of the Associated Press reports that "There is a wide difference in the rates of poverty between racial and ethnic groups 65 and older. In 1998, the percentage of non-Hispanic whites living in poverty was 8.2 percent, compared to 26.4 percent for non-Hispanic blacks, 16 percent for non-Hispanic Asian and Pacific Islanders and 21 percent for Hispanics."[17]

Jon E. Hilsenrath, reporting on an AARP study about a rise in wealth among retirees, also brought attention to a trend that goes in the opposite direction:

> The report sounds an alarm about an underbelly of people heading into retirement unprepared. For about five million, or 15 percent of people between ages fifty and sixty-one— many of them low-skilled workers and many of them women—the trends are going in the opposite direction. Many of these low-income preretirees have already cashed out pensions to cover the costs of their daily lives, so they have little to fall back on. And more of them have no health insurance, meaning they run a greater risk of eating up savings to cover a serious illness.[18]

What an opportunity for seniors to make a difference in the lives of poor children and the elderly by becoming their advocates. It would be refreshing if seniors would become the advocates for poor people. Washington can ignore the few pleas for poor people since very few of them vote. But seniors—that is a different matter.

Seniors advocating for poor people would have two advantages: first, it would bring some real pressure to bear in

Washington and our state capitols on behalf of the poor, and second, it would help remove the impression that many Americans have of seniors today; namely, that all they really care about are their own entitlements.

Political Action

I believe the Vietnam War ended sooner than it might have otherwise because older Americans, including seniors, became involved in political action. Like many others in the early years of the Vietnam War, Judith and I felt our national leaders were correct in what we were trying to do in Southeast Asia. Trying to stop the spread of communism was what our war effort was all about.

Our oldest daughter and son, who were in college, saw it differently. They were part of the student-protest group and before long they, along with thousands of other youth from colleges all across the nation, were descending upon Washington to march in protest.

Judith and I vividly recall watching the morning news on television the day the college youth determined to shut down Washington. Our daughter, Shelley, had advised us that she, along with hundreds of other students from the University of Michigan, were assigned the task of shutting down DuPont Circle, a major intersection in the city. We watched in horror as police shot tear gas into the mass of students and then went in with clubs flailing to arrest them. And our daughter was somewhere in that crowd. That was a scene hard for us to take.

But then came Kent State. The nation witnessed the shooting and killing of protesting students by the Ohio National Guard. That did it for us. Something has gone wrong in our country when our own soldiers are killing our children, we concluded. "It's time for us to march," I said to Judith, and she agreed. There was one peace march in our town, then later a larger one in our state capitol, and, finally, our first march in Washington. The buses that took us to Washington were largely filled with people like us—middle-class, middle-aged people who felt compelled to go.

As soon as we arrived in Washington, we went to the senate and house office buildings to meet with our legislators. Some had escaped by leaving town. The twenty-member delegation of which we were a part met with Senator Arlen Specter in his office. He was hospitable, but clearly did not agree with us. I think he was surprised to see the number of seniors in our group.

We then went to a huge rally in front of the capitol and then began our march. Suddenly the nature of the demonstrations changed. They were no longer the "hippie" crowd: this was middle America marching, and many seniors as well. As we marched down Pennsylvania Avenue, we noted soldiers with rifles on every rooftop. I was not concerned, but even to this day, Judith shudders at what might have happened. The White House was shielded by buses, parked bumper to bumper around the block. The next day, television and newspaper columnists reported on the large turnout of middle-aged and senior people. But the war did not end.

So we went back again and again. The crowds got larger each time. The day Richard Nixon was inaugurated for his second term, we were in the midst of a huge group who had come to protest his Vietnam War policy. Finally, the tide turned and the tragic war wound down to a very sad conclusion. The "hippie" demonstrations didn't do it. It was the mass of middle America on the streets of Washington that convinced our leadership they had lost the support of the nation.

Local Advocacy: Judith's Story

Political action and advocacy on the local level are also an option. During the Civil Rights movement of the 1960s, my eyes were opened to the need for advocacy for the people who are voiceless or suffer discrimination. I had no idea how scary advocacy could be.

Bill and I, in total naivete, agreed to househunt on the Main Line of Philadelphia with an African American Lutheran pastor and family coming from California. A few years before, we had been given the royal treatment by a real estate agent. He spent many hours driving us up and down the Main Line looking at older homes and models. He told us about taxes, schools, churches, and distances to the Main Line Railroad for commuting into Philadelphia.

We happily took our African American couple to this most obliging agent. There was no one in the office to help us. We cooled our heels for a good twenty minutes. Finally, our agent appeared from a back room. When we told him what we wanted, he hemmed and hawed and finally told us to drive around and write down the addresses of homes our friends would like to see. He would then call the owners and make appointments to show the houses to our friends—if the homes were still for sale.

Shortly thereafter we sent word to the many churches on the Main Line that a fair-housing group was forming and the first meeting would be in our living room. Baptists, Lutherans, Methodists, Episcopalians, Unitarians, and Quakers showed up. Some were seniors who had been in previous advocacy movements, but most were in their thirties and forties. A few African Americans, longtime residents but ghettoized in the centers of the towns, appeared to help. All in all, we jammed thirty people in our small living room, most of them having waited for someone to take the first step.

With the antidiscrimination housing laws recently enacted in our state, our job was to find a seller or owner of a rental property who would sell or rent to Caucasians but not to African Americans. It would be a clear violation of the law and therefore subject to prosecution.

A Baptist pastor's wife and I found a young African American couple who wanted to rent an apartment in Wayne, Pennsylvania. They had looked at a particular apartment and were told, despite the fact that it was advertised in the real estate section of the newspaper, that it was already rented. Helen and I went to see the apartment, met with the owner, and agreed to rent it. With the deal made, we immediately reported the violation.

Faced with the threat of prosecution, the apartment owners and the real estate agents reluctantly and, in some cases angrily, caved in. One real estate agent told Bill that he was so glad that he and the rest were forced to obey the law by our fair-housing group. He could not do it alone; the entire industry had to act together.

When Bill was transferred back to the home office, the ugly rumor mill started. Our nice cozy neighborhood would be ruined when we sold our home to African Americans. And who knew how much influence we would have on other neighborhoods?

For me, the frightening part came when Bill was called to the home office to explain his role in the fair-housing group. I did not particularly want to move, but I did not want Bill to lose his job either. The hostility and anger against us was that strong. At least I felt intimidated and somewhat fearful.

Advocacy can be a scary proposition. That's the advantage of being a senior in advocacy. There is no threat of losing a job; in fact, there is nothing to lose.

Corporate Advocacy

Today a large percentage of the senior population is directly or indirectly invested in the stocks of American and worldwide corporations. It may be through direct ownership of stocks or through pension funds that own stocks.

A shareholder, however small his or her holdings may be in a company, is, in fact, a partial owner of that company and has the right to express views on how the company is being run. A shareholder might be interested in such things as the diversity of the work force, a commitment to environmental concerns, good employee relations and practices, product safety, and many other issues. If, for example, a shareholder feels his company is not concerned about the environmental impact of its production practices, he or she is free to write directly to the chairman of the board. If the shareholder feels the response from the chairman is unsatisfactory, the shareholder is free to file a shareholder resolution asking the company to take certain steps to rectify the environmental situation. To do this a shareholder must have owned at least $2,000 worth of the company's stock for at least a year.

A shareholder resolution, if it meets certain tests of the Securities and Exchange Commission, will then be voted upon by all shareholders at the corporation's annual meeting. The company will invariably oppose the shareholder resolution, no matter how good its merits may be, and will seek to negotiate some agreement with the shareholder if the resolution is withdrawn.

In the real world, a person owning one thousand shares of a stock in a company having ten million shares of ownership has no chance of winning the votes of all other shareholders unless the person becomes allied with much larger owners of stock, such as a pension fund. In such a case the large pension fund will be the primary filer of the resolution and it will hope other large funds with major ownership of the company in question will join with them. When the final votes are counted at the annual meeting, a 10 percent vote in favor of the resolution is considered high and company management generally takes steps to do what the shareholder resolution requested. But no amounts of votes—not even 60 percent—can force the company to comply.

Without going into further detail, seniors who hold stocks in various companies are in a position to be advocates for things that make for exemplary corporate behavior. Seniors interested in learning more about their ability to advocate as corporate shareholders should write to the Interfaith Center on Corporate Responsibility at 475 Riverside Drive, New York, NY 10115.

There are also a number of mutual funds that specialize in socially responsible investing. They will hold stock in companies that meet the fund's criteria. For example, they may not be in tobacco, alcohol products, armaments, or other industries unattractive to the social goals of the mutual fund investors. That is the negative screen. Some socially responsible funds have positive screens, such as holding stock in companies that have a highly diverse workforce or are outstanding in product safety or environmental practices.

Socially responsible funds will frequently join with other funds in shareholder resolutions or, on occasion, be the prime filer of a shareholder resolution. Seniors investing in socially responsible mutual funds are participating in advocacy within corporate America.

Advocacy in the public or private sector of American life can add excitement to the senior lifestyle while being of real service to God's people. The opportunities for Christians in their senior years are many. An entire book could be written on each of the lifestyle issues touched upon in this chapter. It is in our lifestyle that we seniors "walk the talk" in putting our Christian values to work. Thanks be to God for the many opportunities we have been given.

chapter
six
work

In his book *Working,* Studs Terkel interviewed all kinds of working people. His short vignettes speak for themselves: people display all kinds of emotions about their work, some love it and others hate it. For some, work is a drudge; for others, it is a joy. Some work just for the money; others find real purpose in what they do. But a comment made by one of the people he interviewed caught my eye. Editor Nora Watson said, "I think most of us are looking for a calling, not a job. Most of us, like the assembly line worker, have jobs that are too small for our spirit. Jobs are not big enough for people."[1]

Terkel found that the primary divide between people who liked their jobs and people who did not was whether they had a sense of personal worth. Whether they sensed a "calling" in what they were doing, as Nora Watson put it.

In the next chapter we will emphasize the role of seniors in volunteering, but there are a variety of good reasons that some will want or need to continue working in paid jobs. But Christian seniors have the opportunity to make certain that they work for the right reasons, and may well have the opportunity to seek work that will also be of worth to others, thus responding to Jesus' call to follow him. This does not mean that seniors should seek work in religious institutions, although that is not ruled out. It means that they should try to seek work in which they can directly serve others. Jesus' ministry was in and to the world. Our ministry in our work should be in and to the world also.

As mentioned in chapter 3, I found five ways to carry out Christian ministry in my work at Bethlehem Steel.

1. Competence is a primary means of carrying out Christian faith in the workplace. Whether we be a carpenter, a shoemaker, a lawyer, a doctor, or a steel sales manager, to the extent that we are competent in our work, we serve others.

2. As we relate to others in our work, we can bring the presence of God into our interactions.

3. It is through our ethics that we express our Christian values in the workplace.

4. When we work to bring about change in unjust or careless policies or procedures in the workplace, we are serving God.

5. Through our lifestyle in the workplace, we demonstrate our Christian values to others.

Those five ways are still important in postretirement work, be it for pay or as a volunteer. As seniors, we should not undertake work with an attitude that we need not take as seriously our senior work as we did our career work.[2]

For the purposes of this chapter, we will use general noun and verb definitions of the word *work*. First, as a noun: "Physical or mental effort or activity directed toward the production or accomplishment of something." And, as a verb: "to exert one's efforts for the purpose of doing or making something." While people most frequently equate work with a paid job, it can also apply to unpaid activity such as gardening, tutoring, performing arts, and creative activity such as writing, painting, sculpting, composing music, and so on. Many volunteer activities can also be work, but they will be discussed in the next chapter. We begin here by looking at the circumstances causing some seniors to work.

Who Will Work in Their Senior Years?

We were having coffee in the fellowship hall of our church. It was December, and I had not seen my friend in a while.

"How are you doing?" I asked

"Oh, fine—I guess," he replied.

"Sounds like maybe you're not doing so well."

"Well, I'm getting concerned about finding a job."

"What's your field?" I asked.

"Like everybody else—computer technology," he said with a forced smile.

"Yes, that could be rough right now. How long have you been out of work?"

"Since May."

"Ouch," I said. "That must be a real worry."

"Yes." He paused. "I'm running low on money and don't know how much longer I can make my mortgage payments."

Gosh, I thought to myself, this poor guy may be headed for bankruptcy. My friend is not alone. The recession that began in 2000 sent many people who once were well-off into personal bankruptcy. A record 1.47 million persons were expected to file for personal bankruptcy in 2001, with an additional 10 percent in 2002, according to SMR Research Corporation, a financial services market-research firm. An article in the *Wall Street Journal* told of William Oakes, who was earning $160,000 a year as vice-president of a software firm. He was laid off in April 2001 with a debt of more than $300,000. Unable to find a job by November, he had cashed out all his retirement funds and had to borrow from his church to meet his latest mortgage payment. His lawyer told him he had to file for bankruptcy.

"I was so ashamed to have to file for bankruptcy," Oakes said. Many of the millions who go into chapter 7 or chapter 13 bankruptcy eventually work their way out. Oakes will probably work his way out, but it will take many years.[3]

Having cashed in all their retirement savings, however, few of the bankrupt individuals will be able to look forward to much of a retirement, if any. The recession of 2000 will mean that some people will have to work many more years than they were planning. It is not a pretty picture. The bottom line of this chapter is that for a variety of reasons presented here and in chapter 9, many people will be working for pay in virtually all the second half of their lives. Some people just like to work. It is not a money thing. Others may feel uneasy about having enough resources to support their lifestyle.

For many people in our society, there never has been a retirement. The working poor, who are earning less than the official poverty level ($8,350 for a single person; $11,250 for a family of two; $14,150 for a family of three; and $17,050 for a family of four[4]) are generally in jobs where no retirement or health benefits are provided.

Journalist Barbara Ehrenreich is among those who say it is not possible to exist at the outdated federal poverty levels. In her eye-opening book, *Nickel and Dimed: On (Not) Getting By in America*, Ehrenreich tells of working as a waitress, a hotel maid, a cleaning woman, a nursing-home aide, and a discount store sales clerk. Her conclusion was that one such job is not enough; that at least two jobs are needed if you want to live with a roof over your head.[5] The working poor tend to move from one employer to another, thus losing the benefit of vesting even if retirement benefits are provided by one or more of their many employers. Social Security checks will be much too small to live on. For these people, work is necessary far into their senior years.

Many working persons have been victims of an early, forced retirement by an employer who has downsized, merged, or even been purchased by another employer. While they may be vested for retirement benefits, their years of service or 401(k) accruals have been far too small to provide a livable pension. Some companies may provide liberal severance packages, but only the highly paid executives are likely to get enough to live comfortably for the rest of their lives. In general, people who are forced to retire in their fifties or younger simply must find another job to provide for their families.

They usually get little help from their former employers. AT&T, which forced 25,600 retirements from 1998 to 2000, gave their former employees free calling cards so they could search for jobs and fax out resumes across the country without charge. Not much help! [6]

Some persons who have been retired for years may be forced to go back to work to make up for the diminishment or even total loss of health benefits when their former employer is sold to another company. In 1992, for example, Chiquita Corporation sought a court order that it had a legal right to reduce medical benefits in its recently acquired Morrell meat-packing unit. In 1994, the court ruled that Chiquita could reduce retiree benefits for some 3,300 retirees. In 1995, Chiquita eliminated all health benefits to retirees of Morrell and sold the company to Smithfield Foods, Inc. Since Smithfield bought the Morrell unit without health benefits for retirees, they kept it that way. The result was that 3,300 retirees, who once had employer-provided health coverage, had to pay for their own health insurance. Many had to find second jobs. [7]

Then there are some who voluntarily took early retirement from their primary occupation to pursue work of a different kind. I am one such person. As explained in chapter 3, I did not want to spend all my life working for the same employer, so I took retirement from Bethlehem Steel at age fifty-six. I received a lump-sum pension that I rolled over into an IRA. Since IRS rules prohibited me from withdrawing from my IRA fund before age fifty-nine-and-a-half, I needed income for daily living. My management consulting company provided that income until age sixty-five when I began withdrawing some money from my IRA.

Another group of people working for pay in their senior years are those who have spent their careers with one or more employers and have been retired by the most recent one with full pension. They work because their pension savings and Social Security checks are not enough to support the style of living they want. Or they may be concerned about outliving their resources. Some may be obsessed with accumulating more wealth.

Indeed, there may be real incentives for the baby boomers to continue working. Gene Epstein, writing in *Barron's*, points out that "by 2020 there will be several million fewer people aged 35–54 than there are today, even though almost surely there will be many more jobs that need to be filled. This will motivate companies to make accommodations to attract and keep employees."[8]

Another reason for baby boomers to continue working is one that few people care to contemplate: the potential collapse of Social Security and Medicare. By 2030 about 20 percent of our population will be sixty-five and older, up from 12 percent in 2001. That represents seventy million people, double the number in 2001. As indicated above, there will be millions of fewer persons aged thirty-five to fifty-four in the workforce. How will Social Security and Medicare be funded? The collapse of these two entitlements seems unthinkable, and yet, what if it happened?

Jobs for Seniors

If, for whatever reason, a senior needs a full-time paying job, the going may be rough, especially if the income level must be the same as the job he or she previously held. This book is being written at a time when the nation's economy has gone into a recession and the stock market has experienced a steep decline. What effect all of this may have on employment opportunities is difficult to assess. What we can do is review the situation that has prevailed for seniors over the past two decades. First, in general, workers over fifty-five have difficulty securing jobs at pay levels equal to what they once experienced. High-tech companies are more averse to hiring seniors than low-tech firms. During the low unemployment years of the 1990s, however, employers with lower-income jobs available began to prefer senior workers over younger people with poor education and a low work ethic. Senior employees typically have a good work ethic, better work experiences, and are reliable.

Bonne Bell, a family-owned cosmetics firm outside Cleveland, has a seniors-only production department that comprises almost 20 percent of the company's workforce of 500. Jess Bell, the seventy-six-year-old son of the founder, launched the seniors-only production department, not as a grand social experiment, but as a practical business move. With low unemployment and a fairly high turnover of new hires, Jess decided to call back some of his retirees. Word got around and before long Bonne Bell had a waiting list of experienced seniors waiting for a job.

The Bonne Bell assembly line staff consists mostly of women, with an average age of eighty-six. The seniors prefer to work with their own age group. "The young ones are too fast and competitive," complained one woman. Another man says, "When you are sixty-plus, you don't necessarily want to listen to the conversation of twenty-year-olds, let alone their music." The seniors fill in for each other and there is a flexible, family-friendly policy. The department is efficient and cares about quality. In short, it works.[9]

Part-Time Work for Pay

Retail jobs that are seasonal or have peak demands at certain hours of the day are ideal for seniors who want to work part-time. The Christmas season is always a good time for retail sales work. Fast-food eateries are happy to have part-time employees for peak daytime demand. For seniors in good health, outdoor work such as gardening, lawn mowing, snowblowing, and so on, is always available.

Our friends Ginger and Dave Fishburn have built up a good business as housesitters for people who go on extended vacations. They move into a house and take care of plants, pets, and phone calls. The Fishburns accept only as many requests as fit into their personal plans. Another friend, Sam Pretz, is an excellent "Mr. Fix-it." He can repair or replace almost anything. Sam accepts only as many requests as fit into his other activities.

The thing that fuels so many part-time opportunities for seniors is the fact that many younger two-wage-earner families simply have no time for work around the home. They work long hours and need to support their children in sports and other extracurricular activities. Sometimes, one of them can cut back to a part-time job in order to provide more support for their children's activities. Or possibly both can take part-time jobs. But mostly they need part-time paid help. Seniors can meet that need.

At our local senior citizen center there are many part-time instructors in computers, painting, dancing, handcrafts, and cooking. Drivers for school buses are always needed, but you really have to love kids to put up with all the noise.

How Much Is Enough?

The lower the need for pay, the more opportunity there is to serve others through jobs having little or no financial remuneration. Which brings us back to the earlier question, "How much is enough?" How much money do we really need in our senior years? Do we worry too much about not having enough money? Jesus says:

> Therefore I tell you, do not worry about your life, what you will eat or what you will drink, or about your body, what you will wear. Is not life more than food, and the body more than clothing? Look at the birds of the air; they neither sow nor reap nor gather into barns, and yet your heavenly Father feeds them. Are you not of more value than they? And can any of you by worrying add a single hour to your span of life? And why do you worry about clothing? Consider the lilies of the field, how they grow; they neither toil nor spin, yet I tell you, even Solomon in all his glory was not clothed like one of these. But if God so clothes the grass of the field, which is alive today and tomorrow is thrown into the oven, will he not much more

clothe you—you of little faith? Therefore do not worry, saying, "What will we eat?" or "What will we drink?" or "What will we wear?" For it is the Gentiles who strive for all these things; and indeed your heavenly Father knows that you need all these things. But strive first for the kingdom of God and his righteousness, and all these things will be given to you as well.

So do not worry about tomorrow, for tomorrow will bring worries of its own. Today's trouble is enough for today. (Matt. 6:25-34)

The word *worry* appears six times in the above quotation. Jesus does not say that we should not work for our food and clothing. We should. But our lives must not be consumed by worry—worry about having enough. And the older we get, the less we should worry about having enough. Senior living should point us away from concern for money and more toward concern for others.

Senior living does not mean an end to work. For a variety of reasons, persons may need or want to work for pay well into their elder years. But whenever possible, Christians should seek that work that best expresses their response to God's gift of years of extended life.

In the Gospels of Matthew, Mark, and Luke, we read the well-known Beatitudes, in which Jesus speaks of those who are "blessed." In the Gospel of Luke, Jesus says:

But woe to you who are rich,
    for you have received your consolation.
Woe to you who are full now,
    for you will be hungry.
Woe to you who are laughing now,
    for you will mourn and weep.
Woe to you when all speak well of you, for that is what their
    ancestors did to the false prophets. (Luke 6:24-26)

With those words of warning, Christians have to be honest with themselves when they ask, "How much is enough for me?" For Christians, the answer must be weighed against the ministries they could be performing in society if they were not working for pay. The rest of this book will deal with opportunities Christians have if all or most of their time is free for nonpaying ministry to others.

chapter
seven
volunteering

Throughout this book, I have argued that seniors can and should contribute to the lives of others. One obvious way to do that is by volunteering. In this chapter, we will look at why people volunteer, as well as varieties of volunteering.

Our county Meals-on-Wheels recently celebrated its thirtieth birthday. The local newspaper ran a feature article on the organization in which it was revealed that five persons have been volunteers from the start. Five people have delivered meals to needy persons for thirty years, at least once a week, sometimes more often. I know four of those five veterans. They all agree: "What we do is a joy."

So it is with Millie, in her eighties, one of a small group of volunteers from our community who weekly goes to a local elementary school to read to young children and help their teacher in any way she can. "I love to be with those little children and help them to learn to read!" says Millie with great passion.

Paul repairs used computers and gives them to low-income families. Martha is the organizer of a community music school that offers lessons on any musical instrument to children regardless of their ability to pay. Jerry is the coach of a Little League baseball team. Hazel offers free childcare to any young mothers in our church who need some time away from their infants for doctor appointments, shopping, or any other need.

After many years of doing volunteer visitation of the sick members of his church, Ellis Valkenburg decided that the family caregivers needed support also. Many of these people were giving care to both their children and their own parents. They were members of the "sandwich generation." Ellis began an organization called "The Sandwich Generation" that provides support for these families with heavy caregiving responsibilities. The remarkable thing is that Ellis is eighty-one and still going strong.[1]

We have scores of friends who are volunteering their services to others and sitting on boards or committees that help to make our community function.

Why Volunteer?

Volunteering has been an important part of American life throughout its history. In our first centuries, volunteering originated primarily with religious organizations. Toward the end of the 1800s, the notion of helping others—particularly the less fortunate—became a part of our civic duty. Today, both volunteering and philanthropy are roughly twice as common among Americans as among citizens of other countries.[2]

Why do people volunteer today? Among the motives for volunteering, a Peter D. Hart survey found that 71 percent of the respondents included "feeling an obligation to give back" as one of the most important. Give back? Give back to whom? Why? The first response to those questions usually is, "I want to give back to society in gratitude for all that I have received in my life." When I press that notion of "for all that I have received," many people will refer to "God's blessings." "God has blessed me so much with a good family, a rewarding career, good health, many material goods, and good friends." "Because I have been blessed far more than I deserve, I want to give thanks to God by serving God's creatures." That's the way many, many volunteers feel, and it is a wonderful example of sensing the grace of God.

This sense of God's grace stands in sharp contrast to the notion of some seniors that "I worked hard for what I have.

Now why shouldn't I be able to sit back and enjoy it?" I have found that this attitude is frequently expressed when I ask people to help with our Interfaith Coalition on Poverty, where we try to get people from welfare to self-sufficiency. With almost no knowledge of the barriers facing these people today, these seniors tend to say, "Look, I remember the Great Depression. No one took care of us. We worked our way out of it. I pulled myself up by my own bootstraps and they should do so also."

This attitude flies in the face of the many biblical admonitions to care for the poor. The Psalms are filled with such reminders. "For the needy shall not always be forgotten, nor the hope of the poor perish forever" (Ps. 9:18). "For he delivers the needy when they call, the poor and those who have no helper. He has pity on the weak and the needy, and saves the lives of the needy" (Ps. 72:12-13). "Give justice to the weak and the orphan; maintain the right of the lowly and the destitute. Rescue the weak and the needy; deliver them from the hand of the wicked" (Ps. 82:3-4).

In the New Testament, Jesus shocks the rich young ruler who has obeyed all the laws of Moses by saying, "go, sell your possessions, and give the money to the poor, and you will have treasure in heaven; then come, follow me" (Matt. 19:21).

The Hart survey showed that the most frequent reason people give for not volunteering is that they do not have time. This may indeed be legitimate for those seniors who must work for income or who are the sole caregivers for a sick family member. But if not having enough time is a result of daily golf or tennis, sitting around a swimming pool, sailing, regular travel, or other self-serving activities, one has to question one's spiritual focus. Is it "I-centered" or "God-centered"? We say hoorah for those who volunteer out of gratitude for all God has given them. They have experienced the grace of God and give thanks by serving others.

Bill's Experiences Volunteering

Where is one's time best spent as a volunteer: serving on the board of an agency or organization that serves people, or directly serving people on a one-to-one basis? I have struggled with this dichotomy for many years, and it still puzzles me at times.

A good example came many years ago as a result of my volunteering to work with young boys who had come under the oversight of the juvenile probation office. I was assigned to two brothers who had several counts of shoplifting between them. There was no father present and the mother was weak at parenting. My role was to be a big brother to the boys, spend time with them, and try to help them stay out of trouble. That volunteer job was labor intensive. The boys were forever asking me to do things with them, some of which I could not manage because of the time needed.

But working with the boys exposed me to our local juvenile justice system. There were aspects of the system that were not helpful for young people. Among other things, I learned how poor people and their children frequently received inadequate legal representation in court. That led to my participation in the formation of the Lehigh Valley Legal Services and serving on its first board. The mission of the organization was to give legal advice and representation in court to people in need. Forming a new organization can also be fairly labor intensive, and it meant less time for my two juveniles. That bothered me also.

Serving on the board of the newly created Lehigh Valley Legal Services organization opened my eyes to many other problems in our justice system. That led to me being named a member of the Governor's Citizen Committee for Corrections, which met quarterly in Harrisburg, our state capital. And as I sat in those meetings, I often wondered if I was really making a contribution to the types of people I once served on a one-to-one basis.

The same thing happened with my church volunteering. My first assignment with Bethlehem Steel was in the Detroit sales office. We joined a Lutheran church in the Redford section of the city and quickly had several opportunities to volunteer. We decided to work with the youth group and teach the high school class on Sundays. We had a great bunch of kids, about twenty in all, and did lots of good things together. It was a great experience for us and our own young children, who looked up to the youth as models. Judith also sang in the choir. Both Judith and I were elected to the church council.

When I was transferred to the Philadelphia sales office, we again joined a Lutheran church in Devon and picked up where we had been with the youth. Again, Judith sang in the choir and I served on the church council. We started a small-group movement in the church and helped to form the Upper Main Line Fair Housing Committee. We became more active in social ministry work.

About eight years later, I was transferred to the Bethlehem Steel home office and again we joined a Lutheran church. We volunteered more frequently for social action causes and I served on the church council. This time we were invited to volunteer for committees of our synod (the name for a regional grouping of Lutheran churches—roughly the equivalent of a Roman Catholic diocese). Soon after, I was nominated to serve on the executive council (National Board of Directors) of the Lutheran Church in America. Much to my amazement, I was elected.

I served on the executive council for eight years and then was elected as a member of a fifty-person Commission for a New Lutheran Church. We were the means for the uniting of the Lutheran Church in America, the American Lutheran Church, and the Association of Evangelical Lutheran Churches into what is now the 5.3 million member Evangelical Lutheran Church in America. I was immediately elected to the national church council (board of directors) for eight years.

From face-to-face ministry with some wonderful kids in Detroit, to boards and committees, to the national church councils: each step took me farther and farther away from the people in the congregations in which we were members. Many times as I returned home from a weekend of national church councils, I tried to tell friends in our congregation what we did. But national policy discussions, reviewing possible social statements, handling constitutional changes, trying to balance the budget, hearing reports on ecumenism, world missions, pension changes, and many others were of absolutely no interest to people in my congregation.

Working with twenty young people in Detroit offered the possibility of helping to shape some of their lives. Working on the national church council of a church with 5.3 million members offered the possibility of helping to shape the direction of a major American denomination. Where is one's time best spent? I have asked that question all my life.

My solution: try to do both. Today Judith and I do face-to-face ministries with Meals-on-Wheels and a welfare-to-work family. At the same time we serve on boards and committees of church, business, and community organizations.

Face-to-Face Ministries

The volunteering Judith and I do that brings us face to face with people in need is done through organizations. For Meals-on-Wheels, we make a commitment for a certain number of days per month on the same route. The frequency of volunteer days can be negotiated with Meals-on-Wheels staff, but commitment is important. At one end is a hot meal, at the other end is a hungry person. They cannot be connected unless a reliable and committed delivery team is on hand. But other than that, little training is involved. For us, our Meals-on-Wheels volunteer work is a response to Jesus' words, "for I was hungry and you gave me food" (Matt. 25:35).

Commitment and reliability are required of all volunteers who work with organizations that utilize them. Whether it is delivering mail in a hospital, reading to children at a school, coaching youth sports, ushering at church, or any other one-to-one ministry, reliability is important. If you do not show up, who does the work in your place?

But not all volunteer ministries require as little training as delivering Meals-on-Wheels, delivering mail in a hospital, or serving as an usher in your church. Some volunteer jobs require extensive training. A good example is our Relational Sponsorship program, mentioned earlier in this book. The program recruits church teams of from two to four people who will help a family move from welfare to work. Ultimately, we hope to get these poor people to a position of total financial self-sufficiency.

A church team must commit to attend training for the job, to work with its assigned family for at least one year, and to meet with its family face to face at least once a week. That's a pretty heavy commitment.

Refusing Pay for Work

I resonate with the wisdom, "Retirement can degenerate into a life of appalling selfishness, narcissism and self-indulgence, but retirement can also make possible a life of loving thoughtfulness and service."[3]

A retired person who doesn't need to work for pay may encounter a situation in which a paying job provides the opportunity to use his or her talents for an organization or cause in which he or she has a great interest. For example, Dick served on the board of directors of a shelter serving people who were homeless. He was supportive of the work being done by the agency. He became chairman of the board and was instrumental in securing ongoing funding for the organization. He did all of this while working in management with a major chemical company.

Shortly after Dick retired from his job, the director of the homeless shelter resigned to take another job. The board of directors asked Dick to become the paid director. Based on his management experience, his passion for the work of the agency, and his knowledge of all phases of the director's job, Dick was an ideal choice. He said he would take the job, but without pay. The board refused because they had to have a paid director. They argued that it would not be persuasive in grant writing if the director was a volunteer. They had to show that there was a full-time spot for a paid director in the budget. Furthermore, the budget would suffer a real jolt whenever Dick decided to leave and the organization had to hire a paid replacement.

Dick agreed to take the paid job, but said he would give his paycheck back to the agency as a contribution. Much to his surprise, the board rejected that, too. The board felt the agency should not become dependent upon the return of a director's salary. It was suggested that he give his earnings to some other causes, but not the agency.

He accepted. For almost ten years he has been working as the paid director of the agency for the same salary paid to the previous director. He accepts annual salary increases, somewhat reluctantly. But his management of the agency, his supervision of the staff, and his continued ability to raise money has been excellent. Some of his former friends are puzzled by his full-time work at a social agency when they know Dick does not need the money. He does not go out of his way to explain his motivation.

Unpaid Jobs

A later chapter will deal with volunteering in society. But there is a type of volunteering that is much like an unpaid job and can provide the opportunity for travel. Here are some examples.

Agricultural Cooperative Development International and Volunteers in Overseas Cooperative Assistance (ACDI/VOCA) is a private, nonprofit organization funded by the U.S. Agency for International Development, and other governmental and private sources. ACDI/VOCA responds to the requests of emerging democracies and developing nations that need help in building businesses or human-service institutions. ACDI/VOCA volunteers may be asked to spend weeks or sometimes months helping a lesser-developed nation build its industries or market its products. The volunteer's expenses are paid by the organization, but he or she receives no pay for the job itself. For more information, visit www.acdivoca.org or call (202) 383-4961.

Our friend Doug Perkins recently spent several weeks in Russia helping the people build democratic institutions. He was working with the Citizen Democracy Corps, which, like ACDI/VOCA, pays expenses but no salary or benefits. Visit www.cdc.org or call (800) 394-1945 for information.

In many local areas, the Executive Service Corps provides free consulting services to local nonprofit organizations. For example, our local chapter in the Lehigh Valley has a board of fifteen directors and a list of about one hundred volunteers with various skills. They receive no pay.

A member of the board who himself is a volunteer gave me several examples of the types of consulting projects they undertake: The Red Cross needed help determining if it should sell the building it owns, or lease it. A senior citizens center needed help in developing a long-range plan, including marketing. A local church needed guidance in developing a long-range plan. Check your phone book or search the Internet for more information about an Executive Service Corps chapter in your area.

Organizations like these require the skills of experienced workers. They provide the opportunity to use the skills gained throughout one's working life to help others in significant ways. A by-product of overseas work is the opportunity to live and work among people of another nationality. It surely beats tourist trips.

Creative Work

We recall that in the Genesis story of creation, "God saw everything that he had made, and indeed, it was very good" (Gen. 1:31). Creation is the result of God's work. Recalling our definition of work as "physical or mental effort or activity directed toward the production or accomplishment of something" leads one to the conclusion that any creative work we do which preserves or extends God's creation is surely Christian work.

The range of creative work is broad. It includes playing musical instruments, singing, and writing music. All three of these skills require hard work to do well. Creative work includes painting with oil, watercolor, acrylic, and other media. It includes sculpting with wood, stone, metals, clay, and other materials. It includes the writing of poetry and prose. It includes dance. All these things help to make God's creation "very good."

My mother, who lived to be ninety-nine, spent her senior years writing poetry for her friends and family. Whenever a friend or family member had a birthday, wedding, anniversary, graduation, or other special event, along came a poem from Hilda. It was a poem specifically written for that person and that person's special event. They were gifts to be treasured. Many times I hear from people cleaning out the belongings of a parent who died, telling me of Hilda's poems that had been saved and tied together with a ribbon. How many people get a poem written just for themselves?

My mother also wrote general poetry that on occasion would find its way into a printed collection. Well before she died, she collected her best verses and had them printed in a small book. Copies of the book went out as gifts to friends from time to time.

Judith's eldest brother, David, is a prolific watercolor painter. Every now and then we will receive one of his latest paintings. No special occasion, really—just when the spirit moves him to share his art with his younger sister. We frame and hang the ones we like most and carefully preserve those for which we simply do not have enough wall space. How many paintings David does before he feels he has a good one, I don't know. But he works hard at his special gift.

Peg Mangum had a house near our summer home in the Pocono Mountains. She had a large open lot surrounded by forest. She spent her senior years gardening. Her beautiful gardens were a delight to see. Not only did Peg provide beauty in the midst of a forest, she enjoyed helping others with their gardening problems. She was happy to give a friend cuttings or seeds to help spread her talent to other gardens. Gardening is work—hard work. But it was Peg's ministry in creative work.

Our son, Bill, who has not yet reached retirement, has a practice of taking his guitar along when he visits people. He never pushes his music making on people but, if the setting seems right, he may softly play the guitar. More often than not, group singing begins and people ask for their favorite songs. He never organizes the singing, he just lets it happen and he plays along. Learning to play a musical instrument can be hard work, but it is a great idea for seniors.

There is a group of seniors in our area who have organized a 1940s-style big band. They are happy to be invited to play for free at dances. A few are former professional players, but most are amateurs who love the music. The band practices weekly. Once a year they have a benefit concert to raise money for some of their expenses, but primarily these seniors love to help others reminisce through their music.

Obviously, most of the creative works in our culture—music, literature, architecture, painting, dance, poetry, and others—are done by persons for pay or, at least, in the hope of being paid. The point here is that creative work is a way in which Christians in senior living can enrich the lives of others through the gifts of their talents, without pay.

The Board Trap

Serving on the boards necessary for all community organizations is another field for volunteers. Boards of directors are needed for social service agencies, service clubs, hospitals, musical organizations, drama groups, colleges and universities, country clubs, parent-teacher organizations, public authorities, clubs, and on and on.

Boards typically review staff activities and set policy for the organization. Board members can be elected by the organization's membership (as in a club), can be elected by the board itself (as in a social service agency), or can be appointed by an elected official (as in a municipal planning authority). Having served on nominating committees of many boards during my lifetime, I can say, in all honesty, that board members are more often selected for what they can bring to the organization than for what life experiences they have that relate to the mission of the organization.

For example, board members of a symphony orchestra or opera are not selected on the basis of their own musical experience. They are selected perhaps as a reward or inducement for a major financial gift, or because they have a high status in community life. The same criteria apply for colleges and universities. As a result, one gains public status by being on such boards. In some cases, high-profile people only give their name to the board; they seldom attend regular board meetings.

Social service agencies generally seek board members who will insure inclusiveness. Such boards need members of both genders, from diverse socioeconomic backgrounds, and from various ethnic groups. A lawyer and a financial expert are frequently needed. Finally, many human service agencies want to have one or two client members on the board. It is hoped that a board with such a variety of members will be better equipped to accurately review programs, staff, and policy.

It is not being cynical to state that a good, well-run organization owes its success to its staff. It *is* being cynical to say that a good staff doesn't let its board interfere with what it is doing. Staff likes to have a "rubber stamp" board that brings in money. Perhaps this is a cynical observation, but too often it is true. It is the staff that carries out the daily work of the organization. It is the staff that sets the course of its work. It is the staff that hires, fires, rewards, or punishes its own members for good or poor performance. The typical board has neither the time nor the expertise to direct the staff's daily work.

The president of the board of directors is the one who is closest to the organization's executive director. The president's role is to be supportive of the executive director and help in any way he or she can. The president may counsel the executive director when he or she seems to be making an unwise decision, but primarily the board president is supportive of the executive director and, therefore, of the entire staff.

I once had a candid conversation with the president of the board of a major community organization about his role. He said, "I run the board. I never let the board vote on any issue of substance unless I know it will come out my way." He added, "Before I take a vote on any important matter I will know exactly how each board member will vote."

What is all this leading up to? Simply this: when we volunteer to drive Meals-on-Wheels, we deliver food to the homes of people in need. Do we change their condition of poor health or poverty? No. Yet these people *do* need food. When we volunteer to serve on the board of a social service agency, do we change the condition of those who are served? Not directly; the staff does. Yet organizations do need boards of directors who, presumably, insure that clients' needs are met.

We should not fool ourselves into thinking that we can always do more for people who are poor and in need by serving on the board of a social service agency than by direct one-on-one ministry. And we need to be honest with ourselves about volunteering on a board that brings us greater prestige. Some people collect board memberships like trophies. They look great in an obituary, but are they truly serving God? Yet, in spite of this cynicism about serving on boards, there are times when, doing so, we can make a little difference.

We Can Ask the Awkward Questions

I was serving on the executive council of the Lutheran Church in America during the Vietnam War. We met for four days, four times a year. During one of these meetings of our national governing body, the secretary was leading us through its constitution. We were deciding where parentheses and brackets belonged. Parentheses are used to explain something; brackets are used to indicate options. We were at this for over a half hour, and I was bored to death. As I put my head down, I noticed on the floor that the front page of the *New York Times* carried a bold headline about our president ordering the bombing of Hanoi.

What we were doing with parentheses and brackets seemed so trivial against what was going on in the outside world. I just couldn't stand it. I raised my hand and was recognized. In an angry voice, I declared, "We have been discussing parentheses and brackets for over a half hour." I raised the *New York Times* above my head and continued. "Look what is going on in the outside world right now! We have never once discussed this war!"

There was silence. No one knew what to say or do. It was an awkward moment. Without responding to my outburst, the secretary cleared his voice and said, "Shall we continue with the constitution?" From across the table came the voice of one of our church's most distinguished theologians. "No, I think not," he said. "Mr. Diehl is right. We have not discussed the war. The highest legislative body in the Lutheran Church in America has been meeting for three days and not one word has been said about this war. I move we table the constitutional work and spend some time discussing the Vietnam War." The motion was seconded and the vote was unanimous.

We shared our thoughts and concerns and out of it came instructions to our denomination's president to send a letter to the thousands of congregations and pastors in our church urging them to discuss and pray for an early resolution of the war. A month later my home congregation received that letter, from the president of the Lutheran Church in America, on the topic of the Vietnam War. It all started because a token layperson on the board of church dignitaries spoke his mind and asked an awkward question.

But such times are few and far between. This story illustrates another benefit of being a senior. Since we are no longer beholden to an employer or any group, we are free to ask the awkward questions. We are free to state our honest positions on any matter of societal concern, either orally in a group or in a letter to the editor of our newspaper. We are free to participate in social action, including marching in protest demonstrations. No one but God has a claim on our actions and it is only to God that we are held accountable for our inner thoughts and outer expression of them.

Volunteer Opportunities

"Ask not what your country can do for you—ask what you can do for your country." Those were the stirring words of John F. Kennedy in his 1961 inaugural address. They are the words for which he is most often remembered. Following are some organizations you might consider contacting to volunteer.

A few months following his inauguration, President Kennedy established the Peace Corps, which celebrated its fortieth anniversary in 2001. Today the Peace Corps serves in sixty-five countries around the world. Host countries prefer older volunteers because they offer experience and maturity. Volunteers are sought in various levels of teaching, in skilled trades, in home economics and nutrition, in agriculture, and in community development. Volunteers are expected to speak the language of the host country and, accordingly, receive intense language instruction. Assignments are typically for two years. Volunteers are supervised and work with natives of the host country. In his State of the Union address on January 29, 2002, President George W. Bush called for doubling the Peace Corps to send 7,000 more volunteers overseas. Further information can be obtained by calling (800) 424-8580 or visiting the Peace Corps Web site at www.peacecorps.gov.

Experience Corps is a project of Civic Ventures that mobilizes Americans fifty-five and older on behalf of children in more than two dozen communities around the nation. Experience Corps volunteers serve either half-time (fifteen to twenty hours per week) in return for a stipend, or part-time (two to ten hours per week), in schools and community youth organizations such as YMCAs or Boys and Girls Clubs. These older adults tutor and mentor individual children and take on special projects designed to enhance the children's education. Some volunteers work to engage more parents in the schools, while others develop after-school activities and build community support for children and schools.

Civic Ventures president Marc Freedman has impressed many observers with the success of Experience Corps. He is the first to concede that it is still a small-scale project, but he is highly optimistic about its potential as the baby boomers move into retirement. "This aging society presents us with a massive opportunity," he says.[4] More information can be found at www.experiencecorps.org.

On September 21, 1993, Congress created the Corporation for National Service to administer a variety of existing federally funded volunteer programs. In fiscal year 2000, its appropriation was $731.6 million. The corporation oversees three major service initiatives, of which two, AmeriCorps and the National Senior Service Corps, offer volunteer opportunities for seniors.

AmeriCorps, the domestic Peace Corps, engages more than 50,000 Americans in intensive results-oriented service. Most AmeriCorps members are selected by and serve with local and national organizations like Habitat for Humanity, the American Red Cross, Big Brothers and Big Sisters, and Boys and Girls Clubs. Others serve in AmeriCorps*VISTA (Volunteers in Service to America) and AmeriCorps*NCCC (the National Civilian Community Corps). After their term of service, AmeriCorps members receive education awards that help finance college or pay back student loans.

Many AmeriCorps grants are awarded through state commissions and other approved entities that submit state plans built on existing service initiatives. Public and nonprofit organizations can apply to the state commissions for subgrants, can implement and operate service programs, and can obtain education awards for eligible participants. National and multistate nonprofit organizations, Native American tribes, and institutions of higher education can apply directly to the Corporation for AmeriCorps funding. In addition, organizations and public entities that manage their own nonfederally funded community service programs can apply directly to the Corporation for AmeriCorps education awards for their participants. All AmeriCorps grants require matching funds. For more information on AmeriCorps, call (800) 942-2677 or check its Web site at www.americorps.org.

The tragic terrorist attacks of September 11, 2001, brought an outpouring of persons asking what they can do to help. Donated blood and money were immediate needs, but people wanted to do more. Sensing the opportunity for offering young people volunteer work in public service, Senators John McCain and Evan Bayh introduced legislation in 2001 that would greatly expand the ranks of AmeriCorps. The proposed bill would continue the current AmeriCorps policy of awarding an education grant (currently $4,725) to each person who completes a year of service.

McCain's goal was to increase the number of future national leaders with firsthand experience in the armed services, closing the worrisome gap between the civilian and military culture. To which David Broder concluded, "In this and every other way, expanded opportunities for national service could be a great response to the September 11 tragedy."[5] President George W. Bush also supported the expansion of AmeriCorps as part of the nation's "new culture of responsibility."

Through the National Senior Service Corps (Senior Corps), nearly half a million Americans age fifty-five and older share their time and talents to help solve local problems. As foster grandparents, they serve one on one with young people with special needs; as senior companions, they help other seniors live independently in their homes; and as volunteers with the Retired and Senior Volunteers Program (RSVP), they meet a wide range of community needs. For more information on the Senior Service Corps, call (800) 424-8867.

Vacation Volunteering

Concern has been expressed in this book as to the degree to which baby boomers would volunteer as they entered their senior years. A promising harbinger is the increasing trend for boomers to take vacation trips where they can help people in need.

"The trips are aimed at travelers who want to come back with something deeper than a tan," said Kevin Long, marketing director of Global Citizens Network, one of several nonprofit travel organizations. Volunteers pay their own way, but frequently stay free of charge in the homes of people they are helping.

"I wanted to do a getaway where it was low budget but was in the spiritual realm of helping others," said a forty-two-year-old massage therapist from Massachusetts.

Susan Carey of the *Wall Street Journal* writes, "This hybrid form of tourism mixed with public service is gaining momentum as baby boomers hit an age where they have the time, resources and desire to give something back to society."[6] Perhaps boomers will be more active volunteers than some people project.

Other Organizations

In the fall of 2001, AARP rolled out a major effort to get more seniors, especially baby boomer retirees, into volunteering. Organizations that joined AARP's "National Call to Service" are:

American Hospice Foundation: Represents hospices that train volunteers for patient care, administrative duties, and other services. Check your local phone book or go to www.american-hospice.org.

America's Second Harvest: The nation's largest domestic hunger relief organization feeds hungry people by soliciting and distributing food and other grocery products through food banks and rescue programs. Visit www.secondharvest.org for more information.

Big Brothers, Big Sisters of America: The nation's oldest and largest youth-mentoring organization, serving more than 200,000 children throughout the United States. Check your local phone book or go to www.bbbsa.org.

Habitat for Humanity: Works to eliminate poverty housing. Check your local phone book or visit www.habitat.org.

Meals-on-Wheels Association of America: Depends upon volunteers to deliver nutritious meals and to maintain social contact with older persons who are homebound. Check your phone book or go to www.mowaa.org.

National Mentoring Partnership: A resource for people interested in becoming mentors to young people. Visit www.mentoring.org or call (888) 432-6368.

Points of Light Foundation: Mobilizes volunteers to do community development work. Call (800) 865-8683 or go to www.pointsoflight.org.

Rebuilding Together: The nation's largest volunteer organization preserving and revitalizing low-income housing and communities. Phone (800) 473-4229 or go to www.rebuildingtogether.com.[7]

The opportunities for volunteering are almost endless. Volunteering is a must for all of us as we move into senior living. It is a tangible way in which we can say thanks to God, who has blessed us along our pathways of life. Matthew writes: "Just as you did it to one of the least of these who are members of my family, you did it to me" (Matt. 25:40).

chapter eight
giving

The years of senior living are not only for giving time through volunteering, but also for giving money. As Winston Churchill said, "We make a living by what we get, we make a life by what we give." Just as we prioritize our use of time in the senior years, we also need to prioritize our use of money.

> He sat down opposite the treasury, and watched the crowd putting money into the treasury. Many rich people put in large sums. A poor widow came and put in two small copper coins, which are worth a penny. Then he called his disciples and said to them, "Truly I tell you, this poor widow has put in more than all those who are contributing to the treasury. For all of them have contributed out of their abundance; but she out of her poverty has put in everything she had, all she had to live on." (Mark 12:41-44)

Jesus was not impressed by the size of the gifts as much as the proportion of the giver's assets. Rich people gave "large sums . . . out of their abundance." The poor widow gave only a penny but it was "out of her poverty."

Why is it that, proportionately, lower-income Americans are more generous in their giving than the wealthy? In my research on giving for a previous book, I discovered that a study done by Independent Sector in 1984 showed that while average giving of all Americans was 2.4 percent of total household income, people with incomes below $10,000 contributed 3.85 percent of their income to charity. Those in the $50,000 to $500,000 range contributed only 1.35 percent.[1]

One might think that the soaring increase in wealth of the 1990's might change that pattern, but this is not so. "The data suggest that lower income groups are proportionately far more generous and reliable in their giving than are America's wealthiest citizens," wrote Joseph A. Grundfest in the *Wall Street Journal*.[2]

It is easy to be misled by the remarkable gifts of the "high-tech nouveau riche" who, for example, in 1999 gave $16 billion to the Bill and Melinda Gates Foundation, or $150 million (from James Clark, founder of Netscape) to Stanford University, or $129 million to DePauw University (from Philip Forbes Holton), or many other multimillion-dollar gifts by the wealthy. The fact remains that, on average, lower-income Americans give a slightly larger proportion of their income to charity than wealthier ones.

The Kern Family

As I drove to the Kern's home, I did not know what to expect. Two of the Kern children, Matthew and Judy, were in the high school Sunday school class I taught. I was not aware if the couple had any other children. I regularly saw Mrs. Kern at worship services; Mr. Kern seldom attended. He was kind of a mystery person. Some people said that he was an alcoholic.

The year was 1952, and this was the first time that I had agreed to visit members of our church in their homes to secure financial pledges for the following year. I was nervous about making visits, and this one was no exception, even though, or perhaps because, the two children were in my class.

My first surprise was the house. It was an old ranch-style home in a rather run-down neighborhood. It needed paint and some exterior repairs. The lawn was full of weeds—where there was any lawn.

Mrs. Kern welcomed me in with a cheery greeting. She had always struck me as a happy person. The inside of the house was neat but very worn. This was obviously a family in need. I was beginning to feel uncomfortable asking this family for a financial pledge, especially when I saw two other smaller children playing in the next room. How could this family of six afford to give anything?

After a bit of friendly chat, I thought it was time to explain the purpose of my visit. "Oh, I know why you're here," Mrs. Kern laughed. "I was expecting someone from the church. I'm glad to meet you. Matt and Judy really like your class."

With scarcely a pause, she added, "We will pledge the same as last year—10 percent of our income." I was overwhelmed and was about to thank her for such a pledge when she added, "I know the finance committee would like to have some idea of what that will be in dollars."

"Well—yes," I admitted.

"I got a raise a few weeks ago. I figure Ed and I can raise our pledge to $12 a week." (Remember, this was back in 1952.)

I gulped in surprise. That was more than the $5 a week *I* was giving! I was quite certain I was earning more money than Mr. and Mrs. Kern combined. I really didn't know what to say other than, "Thank you very much. You are very generous."

"Well, we have always been tithers," she said. "The more the Good Lord blesses us, the more we can give back." She was not boasting or preaching to me, but simply stating the facts as she saw them.

A few years ago, when we were back in Michigan for a reunion of our former church, we met Matthew Kern. He was a Lutheran pastor with two cute little children. He was as friendly and upbeat as his mother used to be. Judy, he reported, was working in Chicago as a caseworker for a social service agency. She also had two children. His mother had died a few years earlier, but not a word was mentioned about his father. It's true. The acorns do not fall very far from the oak tree. Matthew and Judy were in low paying jobs, giving of themselves, but enjoying their callings very much.

We Need to Give

Okay, so what's the point of all this? The point is that as we move into senior living, it is appropriate to examine our financial giving. In the previous chapter, an appeal was made for seniors to give more of their time in volunteer work. One of the reasons was that as older volunteers die or become incapable of continuing in volunteerism, younger seniors and baby boomers are needed to replace them. Well, it is the same with giving money. The older wealthy are dying, and who will take their place? Our society depends on the financial generosity of its citizens to support the many social service agencies that distinguish our nation from all others.

But, apart from the need of our social service agencies and churches for financial support, there is a second reason we should give: "Our church does not need your gift as much as you need to give." That truism should be at the core of every church's appeal for money: the need of the giver to give.

In volunteering, we give of our time. In some cases we have little or no control of that time. As seen in chapter 6, some of us may have to work for pay full time—until we are physically unable. For some people, it is necessary to work two jobs per day. Or it may be necessary to give around-the-clock care for an ailing spouse, parent, or other family member. But we all do receive money—little as it may be.

Much as some of us might say, "I earned my money; it is *mine*," the truth is that we earn our money by using the talents God has given us. "All things come from God" (1 Cor. 11:12) is a theme running throughout the Scriptures. The money we have, no matter how we receive it (legally and ethically, of course), is a gift of God. We gladly receive it, but what we do with it is the next important step.

I don't recall where I first read it, but the illustration of the "two seas" in the Holy Land is appropriate: There are two seas in the Holy Land. The one in the north is bright blue and sparkles. Fish abound in it, and farms and orchards line its banks. Children play along its shores. It receives its fresh water from the Jordan River, which comes from the mountains farther north. It discharges its water back into the Jordan River to the south. It is fresh and alive. It is called the Sea of Galilee.

The second sea lies farther south. No fish can live in it. Nor do farms or orchards line its banks. No children play along its shores. Its water is oily, salty, smelly, and undrinkable. Unlike the Sea of Galilee, which receives and gives fresh water, the sea to the south tries to keep all its water. It is called the Dead Sea. Likewise, Christians need to give, otherwise their faith is dead.

Tithing

Throughout Scriptures, the tithe—10 percent of one's income— is the commonly mentioned way to give. The Bible contains many references to tithing, including:

• "Abram gave [King Melchizedek] one tenth of everything" (Gen. 14:20).

• "Set apart a tithe of all the yield of your seed that is brought in yearly from the field" (Deut. 14:22).

• The people who lived in Jerusalem were "commanded" to give to the priests and Levites so that they might devote themselves to the law of the Lord. "As soon as the word spread, the people of Israel gave in abundance the first fruits of grain, wine, oil, honey, and of all the produce of the field; and they brought in abundantly the tithe of everything" (2 Chron. 31:5).

• In Malachi, the Israelites are accused of robbing God by not paying the full tithe. "But you say, 'How are we robbing you?' In your tithes and offerings! . . . Bring the full tithe into the storehouse, so that there may be food in my house, and thus put me to the test, says the Lord of hosts; see if I will not open the windows of heaven for you and pour down for you an overflowing blessing" (Mal. 3:8-10).

- In Jesus' time the tithe was still the standard for giving. But the tithe is not the only way to show one's love of God. Jesus condemned the Pharisees, "But woe to you Pharisees! For you tithe mint and rue and herbs of all kinds, and neglect justice and love of God; it is these you ought to have practiced, without neglecting the others" (Luke 11:42).

- Jesus also condemned people who exalt themselves over obeying the laws, including tithing, rather than humbling themselves before God. Recall the story of the Pharisee and the tax collector who went up to the temple to pray (Luke 18:9-14). The Pharisee thanked God that he was better than the tax collector since he fasted twice a week and gave a tenth of all his income. The tax collector, standing far away, bowed his head, beat his breast, and said, "God, be merciful to me, a sinner!" Jesus condemned the Pharisee for exalting himself, but praised the tax collector who humbled himself.

When we were first challenged to tithe early in the 1950s at a little Lutheran church in Detroit, it seemed absolutely impossible. To go from the approximate 2 percent per year to 10 percent was out of the question. We were just in the early years of my career. My annual income was not very high. On the expense side, we were paying a fairly high rent on our first house and we had two little children to support. Judith stayed home with them.

The people from the church, however, suggested a way that seemed reasonable. They suggested that we increase our giving by 1 percent every time I received a raise. We agreed. Six months later, I received a modest raise. We went from giving 2 percent to 3 percent. In about six years, we were at 10 percent and decided to keep on increasing for a few more raises.

For those seniors whose total charitable giving (to church and tax-exempt charities) is not at 10 percent, the gradual approach is generally more doable than an immediate jump to 10 percent. Begin by looking at your previous year's tax return. If you itemized your tax-exempt contributions, start with that as a base. If you did not itemize, get out the check stubs for the previous year and total the amount given to your church and other nonprofit organizations. That will be your base. Then, each year add 1 percent of your taxable income to that base and put it in your budget for giving. In a few years, you will be a tither!

The people from our church also suggested that the money for giving be laid aside on each payday. Thus it would be "first fruits" giving, which also is biblical. "The choicest of the first fruits of your ground you shall bring into the house of the Lord your God" (Exod. 23:19).

Paul, writing to the early church in Corinth, said, "On the first day of every week, each of you is to put aside and save whatever extra you earn, so that collections need not be taken when I come" (1 Cor. 16:2).

They further suggested that our tithe not be given exclusively to the church. Citing John 3:16, they pointed out that "God so loved the *world* that he gave his only Son." It does not say that "God so loved the *church*." They emphasized that all the world is the object of God's love and, therefore, Christian charity should go to the world as well as the church.

And so it was that on every payday our family of four—later six—sat around the dining-room table to decide how our tithe should best be used. We decided that at least 5 percent of our income would go to our church. The balance of our tithe might go to various organizations that help people in need, such as Lutheran World Relief, UNESCO, the United Way, the Red Cross, and many others. One of our daughters read about the Christian Children's Fund that cared for children in poor countries. They would assign a child to us and send us a photo of the recipient of our monthly check. We thoroughly checked out Christian Children's Fund and found it to be reputable, and we have continued to contribute to various children that have been assigned to us for forty years. And when our youngest daughter Jennifer got her first full-time job, she called home and asked for the address of the Christian Children's Fund. She began to give on her own.

The defining of the tithe as money given in the name of Jesus Christ but not exclusively for the church is helpful in encouraging people to become tithers. It also emphasizes our ministry in daily life, at every stage of living.

What constitutes money given in the name of Jesus Christ? Different persons will have various definitions. This is how we have been doing it. First, money given to our own congregation and any church-related institution such as an orphanage, college, food kitchen, or homeless shelter immediately qualifies. Next, any sectarian organization that ministers to the poor, homeless, hungry, emergency aid, and so on should be considered. A helpful biblical guide for us can be found in Matthew 25, where Jesus admonishes his followers to care for the hungry, the thirsty, a stranger, the unclothed, the sick, and those in prison.

One secular guide we go by is whether an organization has a 501(c)(3) IRS determination. If so, it is a nonprofit institution and we can consider it. Political contributions and lobbying groups are not included. We do give to political parties and candidates, but the money comes out of personal funds, not the tithe. Gifts of money to family members and friends do not come out of our tithe. If we are aware of a person in need of financial help, we will almost never make a direct gift. (See Maimonides' levels of giving later in this chapter.) Rather, we send money to our pastor or an appropriate welfare organization, designating to whom it should go. Two things are thereby accomplished: first, for the recipient it will be an anonymous gift and second, we can claim an income-tax deduction.

In giving to tax-exempt organizations, it is important to exercise due diligence to determine if the money is being well spent and if administrative costs are low. We will not give to any charitable organization that has more than 15 percent of its operating budget going to administration. Our local United Way has been building up an endowment fund so that in time it can assure donors that every cent given will go for services provided. Eventually, not one penny of a person's contribution will go for administration.

Any nonreimbursed expenses incurred in working for charitable organizations that meet the above criteria will come out of our tithe. For example, our automobile expenses incurred in driving for Meals-on-Wheels come out of the tithe.

The tithe is always a budgeted item in our yearly financial planning. We don't know exactly what our income will be each year (pension, Social Security, consulting, speaking and writing income) but we estimate based on the prior year. Furthermore, since our IRS tax-exempt giving generally runs between 15 and 18 percent each year, we have a budget that assures us of giving at least a tithe.

September 11 Giving

The terrorist attacks of September 11, 2001, in New York and Washington, D.C., galvanized the American people. What could they do? Well, the American Red Cross said their blood banks were low. All over the country people lined up to give blood. So many people came that the Red Cross had to stop collecting blood. As it turned out, little blood was needed after the attacks, but the response of the American people was gratifying and energizing.

Money was needed—money for the families who were left without wage earners. And money poured in, with billions of dollars from the American people—enough to support families for several years and to send their kids to college. The heart of America opened up and people gladly contributed to the cause. It was one way all citizens could respond to the tragedy.

But this generosity came with a cost. Traditional recipients of America's giving were hurt. "United Way of Lehigh County Misses Its Goal for First Time" read the front page of our local newspaper.[3] Many local privately funded social services experienced the same effect. My own congregation ended the year with a deficit.

While America's response to the September 11 tragedy was an outpouring of money, it was not new money by any means. Much of it was in fact shifted away from traditional recipients in response to a great national disaster. All givers have the freedom and responsibility to prioritize their giving. In 2001 they did so, but at the expense of many churches, private charities, and service organizations all over the country.

How to Give

Moses ben Maimon (1135–1204), also known as Maimonides, was perhaps the greatest medieval Jewish philosopher. He wrote extensively about helping people in need. One of his most famous teachings was that some forms of giving are better than others. He defined charity's eight degrees by ranking the forms of giving from the lowest level to the highest. Here they are—with my added examples to make them contemporary.

1. *A person gives, but only when asked by the poor.* I give to a person on the street who asks me for spare change for food.

2. *A person gives, but is glum when giving.* I give to the Salvation Army Santa Claus without being asked, but it is obvious I do it grudgingly because I feel pressured to do so.

3. *A person gives cheerfully, but less than he should.* I cheerfully drop some coins in the hat of a street musician, but not as much as I should to meet her needs.

4. *A person gives without being asked, but gives directly to the poor. Now the poor know who gave them help and the giver, too, knows whom he has benefited.* I take a Thanksgiving Day basket of food to a family I know is in need.

5. *A person throws money into the house of someone who is poor. The poor person does not know to whom he is indebted, but the donor knows whom he has helped.* I secretly slip an envelope of money under the front door of a neighbor in need.

6. *A person gives his donation in a certain place and then turns his back so that he does not know which of the poor he has helped, but the poor person knows to whom he is indebted.* I establish a "special needs" fund with my pastor to distribute to poor persons as he or she sees the need. My pastor tells the recipient that the money came from a fund I established, but that I do not want to know where the money went.

7. *A person contributes anonymously to a fund for the poor. Here the poor person does not know to whom he is indebted, and the donor does not know whom he has helped.* I give money to the local food kitchen fund. The persons who buy and distribute the food do not tell the recipient it comes from me, nor do I know who received the food.

8. *Money is given to prevent another from becoming poor, such as providing him with a job or by teaching him a trade or by setting him up in business and not be forced to the dreadful alternative of holding out his hand for charity. This is the highest step and the summit of charity's golden ladder.* I annually contribute money to a local community college's scholarship fund so that children in need can get good career training.

In this "ladder of giving," Maimonides is sensitive to the feelings of inferiority of those who must ask for help, and the feelings of superiority of those who give help. Christians should strive to eliminate both those feelings as we give to others. In the Bible, Jesus says:

> Beware of practicing your piety before others in order to be seen by them; for then you have no reward from your Father in heaven.
>
> So whenever you give alms, do not sound a trumpet before you, as the hypocrites do in the synagogues and in the streets, so that they may be praised by others. Truly I tell you, they have received their reward. But when you give alms, do not let your left hand know what your right hand is doing, so that your alms may be done in secret; and your Father who sees in secret will reward you. (Matt. 6:1-4)

It is wonderful that in good times, America's multimillionaires can give large sums of money to colleges that, in turn, name a building, a library, or a performing arts center after them. But would it not be refreshing if someday, somewhere, a new building bore the name "The Anonymous Center for the Performing Arts" chiseled in granite over the doors? Today anonymous givers of large sums for buildings merely ask that their names remain confidential, but by using the term "Anonymous" in the building's title, they would also be making a statement about *how* to give. These comments on how to give also extend to charitable foundations. I mention that here because, as we move into senior years, we may be invited to serve on the board of directors of one or more charitable foundations.

The bullish equity markets of the 1990s spawned many new charitable foundations. By the end of 1998, there were 46,832 foundations, up from 23,770 in 1982.[4] Many of these new foundations were established by persons, such as Bill Gates, who want to spread their giving over a long period of time. Most foundations establish a philosophy that guides where their giving will go. This usually is made known to those seeking grants.

For the past few years I have been seeking grants from foundations for an interfaith coalition on poverty, a nonprofit corporation that seeks to help poor people moving from welfare to work. The big, national foundations are not interested in us because our requests for $25,000 are too small. So we are limited to smaller, local foundations. My experience has been that some foundations give only where they are assured of public recognition and, unfortunately, only a lesser number give where they can make a difference without public recognition.

If you are in a position to influence the giving of a charitable foundation, the criteria of Matthew 25 and the principle of not "sounding a trumpet in the streets" (see Matt. 6:1-4) apply to organizational giving as well as individual giving.

Giving through Senior Citizen Discounts

Judith and I have developed a little giving practice that we recommend to all seniors. It began a number of years ago when we were standing in line at a neighborhood movie theater. In front of us was a family with three young children. The kids were dressed in faded, oversized clothes—probably hand-me-downs—and the mom and dad were also dressed modestly, in clothes they had apparently owned for some time. As the mom tried to corral her obviously excited children, the dad slowly counted the dollar bills and loose change required for their five tickets. This was obviously a family in need, out to enjoy an infrequent evening at the movies.

After they left, Judith and I stepped up to the cashier's booth and asked for our usual senior citizen tickets. We were surprised to discover that each of our tickets cost fifty cents *less* than the children's tickets! This did not seem just. After the movie, we talked about the pricing injustice we had just observed. What could we do about it? Perhaps we should stop receiving senior citizen discounts. That might make us feel better, but it would not change the policy. Protesting the policy to the theater manager would not change things either. We were fully aware that senior citizen discounts were given as a commercial incentive. It was not that movies and stores were so sympathetic with the plight of the elderly; it was a way of attracting senior customers. Nothing we could say or do would change the practice.

But we could do something positive. We could give the money saved on senior discounts to poor children. And so, for years we have been doing just that. Judith has a small pad in her purse and records any money we get as a senior citizen discount. When the amount reaches about $50, we send a check to the Fund for Children, a local nonprofit organization. The mission of this organization is to provide money to poor children for things they would otherwise not be able to afford. It goes especially but not exclusively to foster parents. It might pay for the child's class trip to New York or a special dress for a class dance, things not provided for in foster-parent reimbursement.

We thought the idea was so good that we shared it with friends. The general response was, "That's interesting." Wanting to promote the idea further, I wrote an article about how we use senior citizen discounts for our national church magazine, *The Lutheran*. The article clearly states that this idea is for those of us who really do not need senior citizen discounts. I acknowledged that the discounts are needed by some people and are a critical need for seniors experiencing poverty. "It's just for those of us who are well enough off that we really don't need discounts," I emphasized.

The Lutheran immediately accepted and ran the article. "I'll let you know the reader reaction," promised the editor. A few months later, he called me. "The response is mostly negative," he said. "Despite your paragraph explaining that your suggestion is not for everyone, most readers sent in angry letters. The general thrust of the letters was 'Who does he think he is taking away my senior citizen discounts? I earned them and I deserve them!' "

I thought, "Wow! Is this typical of my generation?" Nevertheless, we continued recording our discounts; in fact, we have become aggressive in seeking them out, even on trips to Europe. One time we were about to buy a new range at Sears when we learned that if we came back on the following Tuesday, we would get a 10 percent senior citizen discount. That savings of 10 percent was worth coming back the following week.

About twelve months later, I received a phone call from Laura Sessions Stepp, a feature writer for the Washington Post. "Are you still doing your senior citizen discounts?" she asked.

"Yes, but how did you learn about it?"

"Well, I was going through my pack of clippings I save for possible future use and I came across your article in The Lutheran. Would you mind if I did a feature story on it? My column is syndicated and will appear in newspapers all over the country."

I gladly gave my permission, stating that I was trying to promote the idea. She asked me some questions and about two weeks later, I received a letter from her, enclosing a copy of the article.

In no time at all, I heard from former Bethlehem Steel associates in Tampa, Ann Arbor, Houston, Los Angeles, Albany, and other cities. They all congratulated me on the article, but not one said they were going to try it. The few I pressed on giving it a try said, "We're thinking about it." Most of them said, "Keep up the good work!" I knew every one of these people and I knew that every one of them was financially comfortable. Yet to my knowledge, not one of them began to put aside their senior citizen discounts for giving to poor people. How about you? Do you really need your senior discount? Would you consider saving them to be given to some children in need through a reputable agency?

Dr. Karl Menninger, a renowned psychiatrist, said, "Generous people are rarely mentally ill. On the other hand, let us not be critical of our stingy friends. Remember, stinginess is an illness. Some don't dare give; they might run out. My dear friends, of course you are going to run out. You can't take it with you. The ill individual narrows his vision until he ceases to see the multiplicity of opportunities."[5]

During the Soaring Nineties there was an expression, "He who dies with the most toys is the winner." To which one can reply, "He who dies with the most toys is still dead."

The apostle Paul writes this to the church at Corinth:

> The point is this: the one who sows sparingly will also reap sparingly, and one who sows bountifully will also reap bountifully. Each of you must give as you have made up your mind, not reluctantly or under compulsion, for God loves a cheerful giver. And God is able to provide you with every blessing in abundance, so that by always having enough of everything, you may share abundantly in every good work. (2 Cor. 9:6-8)

The way in which we give of our time and our money is a ministry not only to the recipients, but also to younger Christians who need generous mentors to lead them.

chapter
nine
the
money
thing

The assumptions made in the chapters on volunteering and giving are that there is sufficient financial wherewithal to give back to society in some of the ways suggested. This chapter, therefore, is primarily directed at those seniors (over age fifty) or soon-to-be seniors, who are looking forward to the time when they no longer have to work for a living. This chapter is not a primer on investing or saving strategies; rather, it raises some issues that need to be considered in contemplating the senior years. For that matter, some of these issues may serve as a reality check for those of us already past our working days.

A survey released by the Employee Benefit Research Institute in May 2001 found that "fewer Americans are saving for retirement, fewer are confident that they will have sufficient funds to live comfortably in retirement and fewer have tried to calculate how much money they need to save for later life."[1]

Many people have one major question as they move from their primary occupation into other ventures in life: "Will we outlive our financial resources?" It is a gut-wrenching question with no simple answer, and it all depends upon the lifestyle we want. It depends on how long we will live (no answer), what the future economy will do to our current assets (no answer), what we can depend on from Social Security (no answer), what the rate of inflation will be (no answer), the possibility of a catastrophic illness that will drain our resources (no answer), and the possibility of a severe worldwide depression (no answer). Responses to all those unknowns cover a wide span of philosophies.

At the one end of the range are those persons who really do not worry about their financial future. "We took care of our kids; let them take care of us" is their typical expression. Some of them even have bumper stickers on their cars saying, "Spending our kids' inheritance." These people are not necessarily careless with their assets (although some are); they just do not worry too much about their financial future.

At the other end of the range are the people who want to make certain their assets will carry them through any or all economic possibilities. For many of them, their assets are never large enough. Even if their estate planning is based on a disastrous worst-case scenario of living to be 110, living through a 50 percent drop in the stock market, an inflation rate of 20 percent, putting aside $1 million for a catastrophic illness, and "bunker" resources for living through a worldwide depression; even then, the question remains, do we have enough laid aside? Obviously, some middle ground will be the goal for most seniors. This is where an estate planner can be of help.

It is not within the scope of the book to deal with asset allocation. Entire books are available on this topic. One point on which all financial advisors agree, however, is that seniors should have liquidity in their portfolios that could carry them through at least two years of living needs. But even *how* that liquidity is established is beyond this book.

What are some principles of the Christian faith that may help us decide where we want to place ourselves in the range of no concern about the future to an obsessive concern about the future? Certainly, Jesus' examples and teachings valued people more than possessions. Surely our lifestyle should be the same. Possessions should not play an exclusive role in our future planning; people should. Jesus also preached against being too "anxious" for tomorrow (Matt. 6:25-34).

What these two principles mean for us is that in love for our family and also for those who pay taxes to maintain county homes and other services for the elderly, we should try to have the resources so that, barring any catastrophic illness, we will not have to rely upon them to support us in our old age. At the same time, we should not be obsessed with worry about our future and whether we will outlive our resources.

The traditional method for determining if one has enough assets to last a lifetime has been presented in countless books and articles on retirement. The formula is generally simple: project what you would expect your pension, Social Security, and your retirement portfolio to generate each year, reinvest some earnings as a hedge against inflation, and the rest is available for spending. Or reverse the procedure. Determine how much you absolutely need for your senior living and then see if the combination of your pension, your assets, your Social Security, and your savings income will meet those needs.

The common yardstick used to be that a couple could live on about 80 percent of their preretirement income. That may be bad advice. "Many of my clients end up spending just as much or even more money than they did before retirement," says financial planner Joseph Janiczek of Greenwood, Colorado.[2]

Traditional methods may no longer work, owing to stock market volatility. A sudden bear market can so diminish a portfolio that even a bull market cannot lead to recovery. It may mean that if you need a pension income in your senior years (exclusive of Social Security) of about $40,000 to $50,000, you must have at least $1 million in total retirement assets that adjusts for inflation. A $500,000 nest egg will thus yield only $20,000 to $25,000 income, plus Social Security.[3]

A relatively new way to get a handle on our resources and whether we will outlive them is a sophisticated risk-analysis program named Monte Carlo. All the variables such as stocks and bonds (in varying ratios), inflation, taxes, age at death, purchase of a retirement home, catastrophic illness, and so on, taken separately, can generate a host of different scenarios that effect the amount of money you can spend and still stretch your dollars until your death. Based on the variables, Monte Carlo calculates the probability as to when you will run out of money. By adjusting the variables, you can create best-case and worst-case scenarios that inform your choice about how best to make your money last.

Whether we use a slick computer program such as Monte Carlo, or some other method, at some point we will have to decide how much is enough for us in our senior years. It is important that we be honest with ourselves.

Abundance

Deuteronomy 8 reminds us:

> Take care that you do not forget the Lord your God, by failing to keep his commandments, his ordinances, and his statutes.... When you have eaten your fill and have built fine houses and live in them, and when your herds and flocks have multiplied, and your silver and gold is multiplied, and all that you have is multiplied, then do not exalt yourself, forgetting the Lord your God, who brought you out of the land of Egypt, out of the house of slavery, who led you through the great and terrible wilderness. (Deut. 8:11-15)

We have become so used to abundance that we have lost track of what is enough. The United National Development Programme, 1998 Human Development Report says "Studies of U.S. households found that the income needed to fulfill growing consumption aspirations *doubled* between 1986 and 1994."[4] Imagine, that in just twelve years Americans have doubled the amount of money they feel is necessary to meet their needs.

Much of what has been fueling this "growing consumption aspiration" is the baby boom, which is now at the peak of its earning power and is beginning to move into senior years. Where is the evidence of boomer excessive consumption? Look around you. Look at their cars and their homes. Top-of-the-line sports cars, recreation vehicles, and vans are standard necessities. Not even a fuel shortage slows their appetites for gas guzzling "trophy cars." And look at the houses they are buying. They are bigger and more luxurious than ever before.

"Even luxury builders are amazed at the depth and breadth of the demand," reports Robert Toll, CEO of Toll Brothers, Inc., the nation's largest high-end homebuilder.[5] Houston architect William Stern, who builds just two or three large homes a year, feels that this trend is appalling. The bigger-is-better trend is about "showing off to neighbors," he says.[6] Apart from size, high-end homes pile on amenities such as double ovens, twin dishwashers, and master bathrooms with a Jacuzzi, two sinks, and two toilets.[7]

We are not just talking about Wall Street high rollers. In areas of our town populated by middle managers and professionals, scarcely a new home is built without four large bedrooms, two fireplaces, huge kitchens, and three-car garages. Metropolitan Life estimates that as a consequence, younger boomers have amassed personal debt equal to 95 percent of their annual income.[8]

In fairness, we must say that not all baby boomers have followed the pied piper of exuberant consumption. But enough have been caught up in the materialistic frenzy that it is not unfair to speak in generalities of the boomer generation. The good news is that generation X does not appear to be following in the steps of its predecessor generation. This generation still has time to put more money into savings and less into material possessions.

Social Security

Baby boomers tend to be misinformed about Social Security. In the Employee Benefit Research Institute study referred to earlier, 55 percent of those born in 1960 and later were unaware that they cannot collect one penny of Social Security until they reach age sixty-seven. An additional 21 percent believed they would be eligible for *full* benefits before age sixty-five.[9]

Other surveys have shown that many members of the baby boomers and generation X doubt that there will be any Social Security by the time they leave their paid jobs (see chapter 6). Yet, at the same time, many boomers say they want to retire early.

If baby boomers' saving rate is so poor and if they cannot collect Social Security before age sixty-seven, then how can they retire early? Well, how about pension funds?

Pension Benefits

When I was an employee of Bethlehem Steel, the company had a pension plan that was easy for all employees to calculate. Most large companies had a similar benefit. It was a formula based on multiplying your average income over the past three years, multiplied by your years of active service, and then multiplied by a factor that varied between companies. It was 1.5 percent in my case.

Thus a person who had worked for a company for twenty-five years and whose salary averaged $40,000 over his or her last three years would get a yearly pension of $15,000. One who worked for forty years with an $80,000 salary over the last three years would get $48,000. The above plan is called a defined benefit plan because the amount of pension is based on a formula laid out by the employer, and can be determined in advance. The money to fund the pension comes wholly from the employer. These plans have fast been disappearing.

In a defined contribution pension plan, on the other hand, the employee contributes to his or her own pension fund through withholding from salary. In some rare cases the employer may match the employee's contribution dollar for dollar. The employer invests funds credited to the employee's account and, to the extent that the investments are sound, the retirement account grows. When the employee retires, the money credited to his fund is frequently used to purchase an annuity that will give the employee a guaranteed monthly pension payment.

I am oversimplifying the description of pension plans, but this leads up to an important point. During the 1990s it became quite common for companies to alter their pension plans in ways that reduced their liabilities to employees. Moreover, the long-running bull market of the 1990s led to an overfunding of many pension plans. The reduced liabilities and use of overfunded plans all flowed to the bottom line, where it boosted operating income and increased profits. An in-depth study by the *Wall Street Journal* exposed the many ways in which companies reduce their pension liabilities to the detriment of the employee and to the greater profitability of the company. Using the example of an IBM employee, David Finlay, the *Journal* showed how his employer, through a series of "minor" changes, reduced his annual pension from $71,200 to $57,700.[10]

One of the most common ways to reduce pensions is for a company to reduce the multiplier. In Mr. Finlay's case, IBM lowered its traditional 1.5 percent multiplier to 1.35 percent. But some companies also change plans by calculating the average salary *not* on the three last years of earnings (which are usually the greatest), but on the individual's entire career, thus lowering the average considerably. This is called a cash-balance pension plan, and it has become a popular way to reduce the pension benefit of older workers.

Many employers have provided their employees with a 401(k) savings plan. The usual procedure is that for every dollar an employee puts into the plan, up to a certain limit, the company will match in some manner, say dollar for dollar. The employer engages an outside financial institution to invest all 401(k) funds. In many cases the employee is given limited choices as to where his or her money will be invested. If an employee leaves the employer before retirement, he or she can take all of his or her 401(k) account along to a new employer. The company's contribution may or may not go along. There is nothing to stop a company from reducing its dollar-for-dollar contributions to fifty cents or even nothing.

The unfortunate aspect of employer alteration of pension plans is that they always favor the employer and they are either not revealed to the employees or done in ways that obfuscate the impact. For example, when IBM switched to a cash-balance plan in the mid-1990s, its employees got an explanation that the change was to help "attract, retain and motivate" employees. People like David Finlay were never told it would reduce their pension.[11]

The IBM situation got so bad that employee activists were able to take their grievances to the board of directors at its shareholders annual meeting in the spring of 1999. Alan Crudden, one of the activists, recalled the day in 1999 when he learned that after eighteen years as a professional at IBM, a change in plans had reduced the value of his pension to less than what his wife accrued in eight years as a member of the clergy.[12]

It is unfortunate, however true, that employees cannot rely on company-provided pensions. All the more reason for people to save, right?

Health Benefits

One of the great expenses faced by seniors is the cost of health care. Many companies provide health care for working employees. Some extend the coverage in various forms to retirees. But there is no law to prevent a company from discontinuing the health-care benefit to retirees.

It is especially unfortunate that some companies reduce health benefits after an employee has been retired. In 1994, 3M cut back on payments for doctor bills not covered under Medicare and increased the annual out-of-pocket deduction for retired blue-collar union members from $140 to $1,500. A group of former employees began a class-action suit against 3M.[13]

I had a similar experience as I was planning to leave Bethlehem Steel to start my own management consulting firm, I carefully reviewed the benefits I would get as a retiree. In addition to being able to take a lump-sum pension, I was concerned about health coverage. In my company-benefits book it stated that retirees would be entitled to full health benefits, in accordance with the plan we were presently under. That sounded good, but I took the opportunity to get that statement verified by our personnel manager. Yes, I was correct in my understanding. It was in my printed handbook, he pointed out.

About two years after I left the company, I received a notice by mail to all retirees that there would be a small change in our health-care coverage. It was not a huge change, but it did deviate from that stated in my benefits book.

My chief concern was that if the company could change one thing, it could change everything. I wrote a letter to the chairman of the board, whom I knew, pointing out that the proposed change deviated from my employees' manual. I received no reply. I wrote a second letter; again, no reply. That sent up warning flags for me. I consulted a local lawyer, who agreed that Bethlehem Steel's action constituted a breach of contract. I then contacted a few retired friends at other company locations. They, too, were concerned. We got in touch with a small claims lawyer in Buffalo who said he would represent us at no cost. If we won the case, he said that he would be paid out of our award.

The first step was to get us certified as a class. The "old timers" who knew their way around the company sprang into action. They knew how to secure the names of all current retirees and before long, a federal judge in Buffalo certified that eighteen thousand of us constituted a class action against Bethlehem Steel.

To make a long story short, we won in a federal court in the city of Buffalo. The thing that saved us was that nowhere in the employee manual did it state that the company reserved the right to make changes as it pleased. Without that statement, the judge considered the manual to be a contractual promise to all retirees. The company was ordered to provide us with a health-care plan that he then sealed as a court order. It has been known as the Bethlehem Permanent Health Plan and has been a savior for many widows and elderly people.

Immediately after our victory in court, Bethlehem Steel and hundreds of other companies revised the language in their employee-benefits handbook to include a statement that the company reserved the right to change any of its benefits "at will."

The warning for those soon-to-retire workers and all seniors: Do not count on any printed promise in your employee handbook. Somewhere in the materials you receive from your employer are words to the effect that the company reserves the right to change any benefit at will.

An ironic postscript to the story of our class-action victory is that Bethlehem Steel went into bankruptcy in 2001 and, at the time of this writing, it appears that all retirees will lose all their health benefits. Not even our court order can guarantee retiree health care.

Judith and I turned to a planning expert a second time in our lives when we decided we needed to do estate planning. The importance of having an estate plan was driven home to us when one of Judith's brothers died. Here is Judith's story.

An Estate without a Plan

Bill and I updated our wills periodically. But the need to do some serious estate planning, with our wills as part of it, was precipitated by the sudden death of my next older brother, Ed. He had never married and died intestate, or without a will, creating a myriad of problems for his heirs.

Ed was probably the most intellectual of my brothers. He taught in the English departments of Rutgers, the University of West Virginia, Cornell, and finally the University of Kansas. Living on an English professor's salary, he drove secondhand cars, owned one suit, and spent most of his money collecting. In addition to books, he collected classical music and records, paintings, and all sorts of oddments that struck his fancy. But his passion, as a collector, was Australian aboriginal art and artifacts.

Ed had been a Fulbright exchange professor to the University of Adelaide in Australia in the early 1960s and was fascinated with the bark paintings he saw in museums and secondhand shops. He bought some, and later purchased an entire collection of art and artifacts that included wood carvings, boomerangs, barks, and didgeridoos, all of which occupied various spaces in his apartment. Spending the night as a guest meant clearing a bed of barks and other objects before climbing in between the sheets.

After our mother's death in 1972, Ed assumed, with one of our nephews, half ownership of the Ruhe family farm. As he began to suffer from chronic bronchitis and emphysema, Ed hired a lawyer and started on a will. According to conversations with him over many months and with copious jottings found among his papers after he died, he simply could not resolve the dilemmas of what to do with his aboriginal art collection and his half of the family farm— and I suppose, like the rest of us, he thought he had plenty of time to finish his will.

The heirs of Ed's estate included three brothers, six nieces and nephews, and me. None of the heirs lived in Kansas, and I was the only one living in Pennsylvania, the site of the farm.

Upon Ed's death we had to find a lawyer in Lawrence, Kansas—fast. Everything in the estate had to be appraised. The IRS demanded the estate tax within nine months. The unexpected crunch came with the realization that the Australian aboriginal art collection was extremely valuable. How valuable? It turned out to be the best private collection in the world. I am sure Ed either knew or suspected this, but none of the heirs did. We literally had to search the world to find an appraiser.

The heirs agreed to let me handle Ed's share of the farm. What should have been an easy transaction with our half-owner nephew buying out Ed's share turned into a nasty family split. The details are too painful and disillusioning to share. By the time the farm was settled, the art collection sold, and the remainder of the estate dispersed, five years had passed. And the taxes on the estate—individual shares, estate and state—

equaled 60 percent of the total! It seems that this could have been avoided.

Bill and the Estate Planner

In our first meeting with our estate planner, we were asked to name our long-term objectives. I said that I did not ever want to be financially dependent upon our children.

"Fine," he said. "Let's look at your long-term health insurance."

"We don't have any."

"You don't have any?" he said in surprise.

"No, I've always felt we could self-insure for long-term health expenses. Our short-term health coverage is very good."

"Well, how do you know you have enough financial assets to cover catastrophic or long-term illness?"

"I guess I don't," I replied. So at the top of our list of things to do we put "Get long-term health insurance." We investigated several companies and went through the in-depth medical examinations. Because of Judith's postpolio condition, we could not get the most favorable rates. The quotations we got were shockers. At age seventy, long-term health insurance is expensive. Furthermore, there are exclusionary periods, co-pay requirements, and inflation considerations, all of which we would have to cover ourselves.

That's when we took a second look at Luther Crest Retirement Community. They offered three plans, the most expensive of which included all costs for assisted living and skilled nursing care on the premises. The cheapest plan involved fee-for-service for all medical needs. The difference between the fee-for-service plan and the comprehensive plan was about equal to the cost of the long-term health insurance quotations we had received. Luther Crest's comprehensive plan, however, had no exclusionary periods, no co-pays, and no inflation premium. Clearly, it was a better coverage for us. Moreover, a Luther Crest accountant gives us an annual accounting of the costs that represent our health-care insurance, to be included with our income tax.

Living at Luther Crest is expensive, but we maintain that it is our gift to our children. Not only will we not need their financial assistance, but they will not have to drive many miles to look after us, as Judith did with her mother. And they will know we are in a community where we are well known and well cared for. That was step one with our estate planner, but much more followed.

With the help of computer programs, estate planners can make all kinds of marvelous projections. As indicated in the beginning, we made certain assumptions. We assumed the amount of money we would need to live on each year. We assumed an annual rate of return on our IRA portfolio (which was my lump-sum retirement payout from Bethlehem Steel). We also assumed a rate of inflation for the future. Into all this we incorporated the bequests to children and organizations in our wills. The computer ground up all the data and concluded that our assets would be exhausted at age ninety-three for the second of us who would die. It was interesting to see how a change of only a 1 percent return in my IRA portfolio would raise or lower our age ninety-three assets exhaustion.

Our estate planner also helped us with ways to minimize the estate tax implications upon our deaths. We paid our estate planner a flat fee, which insured his objectiveness. He had nothing to sell. Some estate planners have things to sell: insurance, portfolio management, or investment services. They can be good planners, but one wonders how objective they will be. We recommend the professional services of an estate planner. Your future is too important for you to do on the back of an old envelope.

A Return to Our Estate Planner

We entered Luther Crest, as planned, the stock market performed better than we had projected for our plan, and inflation was very low. Our plan was working well. The economy began to soften in early 2000 and the stock market along with it. By the end of the year the return on our investments in stock mutual funds had dropped into negative territory. Naturally, I was concerned about that. The country headed into a recession in 2001 and the stock market continued to drop. I became more concerned.

And then came September 11, 2001. The stock market "tanked" and business conditions got worse. As a result of the terrorist attacks, the travel industry also went into the tank. Airlines and hotels were particularly heavily hit. A massive government subsidy was needed to keep the airlines in operation. Retail sales going into the Christmas season were off from previous years. All of these things sent us back to our estate planner for a review.

When we plugged our current assets, current expenses, and current rates of return on our assets into the computer, we got a nasty surprise. Instead of our retirement assets lasting until age ninety-three of the "second to die," it had dropped to age eighty-seven. As we looked at our estate planning model of five years earlier and compared it to conditions in late 2001, we discovered that our retirement assets were lower, our return on those assets were lower, and our budgeted expenses were higher. The only good thing was that inflation was lower than projected. Our expenses were higher due to annual gifts to our children, sharply higher medical and pharmaceutical co-pay costs, an unexpected rate increase at Luther Crest, and more travel than we had contemplated.

We made some changes in our investment portfolio (which we had neglected), drew up a new expense budget, and settled for a lower rate of return. The computer then showed us having resources to carry us through age ninety of the second to die. Of course, as we age, the expenses for travel and living costs will decrease, but we have not yet taken that into consideration.

We were guilty of some classic mistakes made by seniors. Other classic errors committed by seniors include:
- failing to consider long-term health-care needs
- failing to consider the effect of inflation and taxes
- making large loans to family and friends
- overmanaging a retirement portfolio
- taking too much risk with investments
- underestimating life expectancy[14]

The Working Poor

Up to this point we have been dealing with those fortunate persons who have, or probably have, enough financial resources to carry them through to the end of life—provided their lifestyle is not one of continuous excessive consumption. But that is not the real world for all of us. Although the economic boom of the 1990s pushed unemployment to its lowest level in decades, many full-time workers were earning 8 percent less in 1998 than in 1972, if inflation is considered. The conference board of the U.S. Department of Commerce reported that 2.8 million Americans with full-time jobs—people working at least thirty-five hours a week, fifty weeks a year—were living below the poverty level in 1998, the most recent year available.[15] That meant that 2.9 percent of all full-time workers were poor. During the 1970s, the poverty rate for full-time workers hovered around 2 percent.

The nature of poverty has changed. In the 1960s, when Lyndon Johnson declared his war on poverty, low-income Americans were older, more rural, and overwhelmingly African American. Roughly 30 percent of the elderly were poor in 1966. By 2000 that number had dropped to 10 percent. In 1966, 50 percent of the poor lived in rural counties, particularly in the South. By 2000 that number had dropped to 22 percent. Instead, 43 percent of the poor lived in cities by the year 2000. In short, poverty is found more among younger, urban people. The fastest growing segment of poverty in 2000 is among families headed by single women. In 1960, it was 21 percent; by 2000, it was slightly under 50 percent. The poverty rate is almost six times higher for single-parent families headed by a woman than it is for those with two parents.[16]

What is most serious for low-income workers with respect to retirement is that they have built up no assets. The employers for whom they work seldom have pension plans, 401(k) savings plans, or even health insurance. A small number of working poor are paying off a mortgage on a modest house, but that asset will hardly fund a pension plan. For the working poor, talk of retirement is nonsense.

No Guarantee

There has been much criticism in this chapter about the baby boom and boomers' lack of preparation for their senior years. Yet those of us already in our senior years must admit that there are no guarantees in financial planning. The sharp stock-market decline, which began in mid-2000, has had a negative impact on many well-planned assets for senior living. The fall in interest rates, as "The Fed" tried to minimize a recession, also hurt interest-sensitive investments. The golden years lost their luster for some seniors about to retire from their workplaces.

Frankly, our own financial plan has hit several big bumps in the road. But we have to be patient and not panic. Our estate plan is fundamentally good. Christians living in all income ranges will have to consider seriously what is and is not necessary for fruitful living in their senior years, which we discussed in chapter 5.

Jesus told the twelve disciples, as he sent them out into a dangerous world, to be "wise as serpents and innocent as doves" (Matt. 10:16). So it is for Christians today as we contemplate our resources for senior living. We do our best to plan our financial resources responsibly, but there is no guarantee for the years ahead. The Lord has safely brought us this far and we trust God will provide for the future.

chapter
ten
that
time
of year

That time of year thou mayst in me behold,
When yellow leaves, or none, or few do hang,
Upon those boughs which shake against the cold,
Bare ruin'd choirs where late the sweet birds sang.
—William Shakespeare, Sonnet 73

Senior living is meant to be joyful, useful, happy, and fulfilling. But ultimately, each of us will die. When, we do not know. Where, we do not know. How, we do not know. In this chapter, we will deal with how we view death, how we help others in grief, and the steps we should take for our own death.

How Do We View Death?

> So live that when thy summons comes to join
> The innumerable caravan, which moves
> To that mysterious realm, where each shall take
> His Chamber in the halls of death,
> Thou go not, like the quarry-slave at night,
> Scourged to his dungeon, but, sustained and soothed
> By an unfaltering trust, approach thy grave
> Like one who wraps the drapery of his couch
> About him, and lies down to pleasant dreams
> —from "Thanatopsis" by William Cullen Bryant

Such is the way in which the poet William Cullen Bryant views death: "By an unfaltering trust" he approaches his grave. Trust in what? Trust that, thankfully, this is his last sleep of sleeps? Or trust that there is an awakening from his "pleasant dream"?

Is death the end? At many points in the Old Testament, the answer to that question appears to be yes, death is the end. The psalmists are particularly clear on this point.

> For all our days pass away under your wrath;
>   our years come to an end like a sigh.
> The days of our life are seventy years,
>   or perhaps eighty, if we are strong;
> even then their span is only toil and trouble;
>   they are soon gone, and we fly away. (Ps. 90:9-10)

> As for mortals, their days are like grass;
>   they flourish like a flower of the field;
> for the wind passes over it, and it is gone,
>   and its place knows it no more." (Ps. 103:15-16)

Why is it, you may ask, that in the Gospels we read of a lawyer asking Jesus, "What must I do to inherit eternal life?" (Luke 10:25)?

And how about the story of Lazarus and the poor man who died and went to Abraham's side (Luke 16:19-31), or the story of the Sadducees "who say there is no resurrection," and Jesus who spoke of "children of the resurrection" (Luke 20:27-38)?

The answer is this: the Old Testament, as commonly found in the Bible, consists of a body of literature spread over a period extending from the twelfth to the second century before Christ. However, Jewish writings after the second century B.C. and prior to the writings of the New Testament do indicate a belief in life after death. Some of these writings can be found in the Apocrypha.

The New Testament, with its conviction in the resurrection of Jesus, is remarkably clear on the topic of immortality. Jesus is quoted as saying, "Do not let your hearts be troubled. Believe in God, believe also in me. In my Father's house there are many dwelling places. If it were not so, would I have told you that I go to prepare a place for you?" (John 14:1-2).

St. Paul was especially clear about life after death. In his letter to the Christians in Rome he wrote, "If we have died with Christ, we believe that we will also live with him" (Rom. 6:8). In the same letter, he also wrote: "For I am convinced that neither death, nor life, nor angels, nor rulers, nor things present, nor things to come, nor powers, nor height, nor depth, nor anything else in all creation, will be able to separate us from the love of God in Christ Jesus our Lord" (Rom. 8:38-39).

In the First Letter of Paul to the Corinthians, he devotes much of his writing to the resurrection. Among other things, Paul writes:

> When this perishable body puts on imperishability, and this mortal body puts on immortality, then the saying that is written will be fulfilled:
> "Death has been swallowed up in victory.
> Where, O death, is your victory?
> Where, O death, is your sting?" (1 Cor. 15:54-55)

Death is not an end in itself; rather, it is a transition from a mortal life to an immortal one. That conviction must drive the way we help others grieve over departed loved ones and the way in which we face our own death. Without the Christian understanding of death, the senior years can become increasingly unhappy, uncreative, unproductive, and purposeless. Increasingly, time will be spent trying to delay death. Why shouldn't one fight death if it is the end—if nothing else lies beyond? With the Christian understanding of death, the senior years can be filled with happiness, creativity, and productivity. Debilitating physical problems can be accepted calmly, knowing that something better awaits us beyond.

Aging

Despite the Christian certainty that death is simply a part of life and that there is an afterlife, most of us want to continue in this life as long as possible. It is interesting to note that while most of us hope for a long life, we do not look forward to getting old.

The fact of the matter is that the number of our days, as described by the Old Testament psalmist, has changed very little over the centuries—"seventy years or perhaps eighty." A baby born in affluent North America or Western Europe today can expect to live to seventy-five to eighty years. In the middle of the eighteenth century in Western Europe, however, life expectancy at birth averaged only about thirty years.[1] The wealth of a nation has much to do with life expectancy. There is a significant and shocking disparity between first world societies and developing countries.

Life expectancy is based on averages. Because of illness, plagues, malnutrition, wars, physical drudgery, and accidents, few people lived to see age eighty in the eighteenth century. Life expectancy was low. But in today's affluent societies with better health care, better food, fewer habits such as excessive drinking and smoking, a safer environment, and less debilitating work, more people reach the eighty-year high of the ancient psalmist. Life expectancy has increased.

Barring accidents—which do become more common as we age—most people can now live until they encounter one of the two most common afflictions of old age: cardiovascular disease and cancer. And even these diseases are losing their grip on us as newer drugs and treatments appear more frequently.

In order to be among those likely to live well into our eighties, we have to follow the rules that help us to cope with the natural aging process of the body. The most common chronic ailments of aging are arthritis, dementia, osteoporosis, urinary incontinence, failing eyesight, loss of hearing, and congestive heart failure. Each of these ailments call for specific treatments but, in general, the characteristics of healthy senior living are a healthy diet, regular exercise, abstaining from tobacco products, moderation with alcohol, and strict weight control. Health magazines abound with advice for dealing with aging. But, ultimately, people die. And with the death of friends and family comes grief.

Grief

Grief comes in many forms and intensities and results from many kinds of loss. The loss of a job, the end of a marriage, the experience of seeing our youngest child leaving home, the loss of friends if we are required to move, retirement from a career—all these losses bring some degree of grief. But the death of a friend and the death of a spouse or close family member brings the deepest of grief. Grief comes to everyone; it is inevitable.

For many years, Granger Westberg's book, *Good Grief*,[2] has been widely accepted as the best guide for helping others deal with their grief. Dr. Westberg suggested ten stages of grief, starting with "shock" and culminating with "affirming reality." Westberg hastens to say that people in grief do not necessarily pass through all ten stages, nor do they experience them in the same sequence he lists. Since first reading *Good Grief* almost forty years ago, I have taken a few courses and read other books on the topic. I have also, inevitably, experienced my share of loss. What follows is a synthesis of what I have learned about grief.

Grief is a complex process. The grieving person moves from an old reality (before a loss) to a new reality (living with the loss). At first, the grieving person evades the loss of the old reality through disbelief, numbness, shock, and denial. But as the grieving person begins to face the new reality of life without the loved one, he or she experiences many effects. In a video titled *To Touch a Grieving Heart*, these effects are grouped into emotional, physical, intellectual, social, and spiritual categories.[3]

The emotional effects include crying. The need to cry wells up within one and needs to be openly expressed. Granger Westberg urges that we raise our male children to understand that crying is not a sign of weakness. He points to the many accounts in the Bible where men shed tears over an event. The shortest verse in the New Testament is the very pointed sentence, "Jesus wept" (John 11:35). We need to help our male friends to express the natural emotion of crying without feeling embarrassed. Sadness and loneliness are other normal emotional experiences.

The physical effects of grief can take many forms. As a clergyman working in a medical center, Dr. Westberg worked with many patients with ongoing headaches, backaches, and "all kinds of aches." He began to ask his patients if they had experienced any serious loss recently—the death of a loved one, divorce, loss of job, last child leaving home, and others. "I have slowly become aware of the fact that many of the patients I see are ill because of some unresolved grief situation."[4]

Depression is quite common with grieving persons and can become deep if they get stuck in working their way through the grieving process. Professional help should be sought. Other physical manifestations of grief can be excessive use of alcohol, overeating, starving oneself, and staying in bed for long hours.

The intellectual effects of grief can sometimes show up in guilt. Guilt that I did not love my partner enough. Guilt that had I protected my child more, she would not have drowned. Guilt that I was not at the hospital when my father died. Fortunately, Christians know that where there is a feeling of guilt there is also forgiveness, and guilt should not be a lingering condition.

Sometimes anger and resentment can develop within the grieving person. Why did Mother die so young and leave us like this? I'll never forgive Fred for leaving me for another woman. Why didn't they fire Jim instead of me? Like guilt, anger and resentment must ultimately give way to forgiveness.

The social effects of grief frequently involve separating oneself from friends and even other family members. The widow is now a single person among friends who are all couples. The unemployed person feels a failure among friends who are working. The mother whose last child has left home cannot bear to be with families whose children are still at home. These feelings can lead to loneliness and sadness unless the grieving person is able to work through the grief process.

The most frequent spiritual effect of grief is to doubt that there is a loving God. Why weren't my prayers answered? Would a loving God permit my child to suffer and die as God did? Why did God take such a fine woman? With the help of friends, family, and possibly a professional counselor (pastor or psychiatrist), most people can work their way through the grief process. But it takes time.

For years I avoided visiting people in grief because I did not know what to say. I was afraid I might say something that would make it worse for the grieving person. "You don't have to say anything," Judith frequently chided me. "Just be there."

Well, once again Judith was right. All the experts on grief agree that it is important that the grieving person knows someone is there for them. If they want to talk about the loved one, join with them. If they want to reminisce, listen to them. If they want to show you pictures, delight in them. Just be present and available. For transportation, for food, for going to church, for receiving telephone calls from them at all hours of the day or night—and listen.

Grief experts are pretty well agreed on things that are not helpful to say to a grieving person. Here are some typical unhelpful statements, along with an idea of the griever's inner response to illustrate why the statement does not help.

- "I know how you feel." *No person can know exactly how I feel.*
- "You will soon feel better." *I just know how I feel now; I'm not concerned about how I will feel sometime in the future.*
- "You wouldn't want [your loved one] to see you cry." *I don't care.*
- "It's good he didn't suffer." *Yes, but he's gone, and I want him back.*
- "You're handling this so well." *But I am crying inside.*

It is also best to avoid statements such as "God is just testing your strength" and "It must have been God's will." These statements are unhelpful and potentially harmful to a person experiencing grief, and should be avoided. Also, avoid the use of "shoulds"; that is, "You should do this" or "You shouldn't do that." So what is left to say? You got it—do not initiate anything. Listen to the griever and do what they want you to do.

How We Can Help Our Loved Ones before We Die

Pastor Diane Karaha, the chaplain at Luther Crest, has experienced grief counseling with residents and their families. She finds that when one of our residents dies, the family must make quick decisions, which puts them under stress especially because they never thought about them in advance. According to Pastor Diane, there are things each of us can do to help our family in grieving over our death:

1. Be sure your will is up to date. Review it from time to time and revise it when necessary. Give the latest copy to your attorney, your pastor, or a close friend.

2. Name someone, probably a family member, to have your durable power of attorney.

3. Complete an advance medical directive, and give your physician, your attorney, and your pastor a copy.

4. Indicate if you want to be an organ donor.

5. Determine if you want a funeral or a memorial service. Determine where it will be and who will conduct it.

6. Do you want an open or closed casket? Pastor Diane suggests an open one so that your friends can see you when they say good-bye.

7. Do you want to be cremated or buried?

8. Do you want visiting hours or a wake of some sort? Pastor Diane suggests some event where friends and family can gather to share memories of your life.

9. Do you have a cemetery lot and advance payment for a headstone?

10. Have you paid in advance for your funeral and casket? It will save your family from being pressured to pay more for your funeral than you desire.

11. Is there a place where all your valuable papers and documents are stored? Does the family know where?

Pastor Diane suggests that all of these things be done before you reach age sixty-five. Sixty-five? Why, I'm going to live well past sixty-five! Oh, yeah? You probably will, but these are not the things you do one month before you die, and *when* will that be? If we take care of these things, we will make things easier for our grieving family.

Judith and I have done all the above except to pay for the funeral director and the casket. We have selected a gravesite in a cemetery in West Allentown. It is a location where once there was a field where my pals and I used to play cowboys and soldiers. The field has since been taken over by an adjoining cemetery. I rather like the idea of being buried under the sod where I used to play as a boy.

Judith adds: In keeping with my passion, I have written instructions for my memorial service in our church. I want our jazz musicians to play. I would like friends and family members to speak—as many as are moved to. Most of all, I want inclusive language throughout the service. I even have a revised Psalm 23 included in my instructions. I may be unsuccessful in changing the male language of our liturgy, but in my memorial service I hope to gain a small victory. There will be many stories and much singing. I wish I could be there.

Palliative Care

A good friend of ours, Dr. Joseph Vincent, has made the promotion of a greater understanding and practice of palliative care a central part of his career. Palliative care involves pain control, but more than that. It involves care for the whole person during the dying process. "The focus isn't cure or treatment but rather comfort and compassion," says Dr. Russell Portenoy, chair of the Pain Medicine and Palliative Care Department at Beth Israel Medical Center in New York. Comprehensive palliative care teams include psychologists, social workers, and clergy members who help patients deal with depression, anxiety, fear, and spiritual issues.[5]

Joe Vincent's concern is that so many medical schools still educate future physicians on curing patients with little attention to pain control and comprehensive palliative care. Can pain truly be alleviated? Dr. Ira Byock, former president of the American Academy of Hospice and Palliative Care Medicine, writes: "Eighteen years of clinical hospice experience has taught me that physical distress among the dying can *always* be alleviated."[6]

The city of Missoula, Montana, has a project called the Quality of Life's End, which educates local doctors, lawyers, clergy, and students about what it means to die well. Both of Missoula's hospitals treat pain as a fifth vital sign, ensuring that medical staff will take it seriously.[7]

Although an increasing number of medical schools are beginning to teach pain control and palliative care, the chief task facing Joe Vincent is how to reach and teach the overwhelming number of practicing physicians who were never educated on the topic.

Dr. Sherwin B. Nuland, author of the best-selling book *How We Die*, writes: "Death is not a medical event. Death is a personal event. It belongs to the dying. It doesn't belong to the doctor."[8] Friends and family of one who is approaching death must be the firm advocates for palliative care for their loved one. Patients alone can not always talk their attending physician or surgeon into securing such care.

Hospice

Hospice is a special way of caring for people who are terminally ill, as well as their families. This care involves physical care and counseling. Hospice care is given by a public agency or private company approved by Medicare. It is for all age groups, including children, adults, and the elderly during their final stages of life. The goal of hospice is to care for the patient and the patient's family, not to cure an illness.

A person qualifying for hospice can get medical and support services such as nursing care, medical social services, doctor services, counseling, homemaker services, drugs, medical supplies, and other services. In order to enter a hospice program, a doctor must certify that the patient probably has less than six months to live. Should a person live longer than six months, hospice care may continue as long as the doctor certifies the patient is terminally ill.

Several years ago a friend of ours was certified to receive hospice care. Friends and family paid regular visits to see Betty, but she continued to live. Much to the surprise of her doctor, Betty improved and she was taken off hospice care. That was two years ago. She can go back into hospice care whenever her doctor certifies she is terminally ill, but at this point the doctor really cannot determine if she has less than six months to live. Betty chuckles over this.

A very attractive feature of hospice is that a terminally ill patient can be transferred home to await death. It is generally necessary to have a primary caregiver available. This can be a family member or a hired person. Hospice also provides "respite" services so that the primary caregiver can run errands or have some social contact with others. Caring for a bed-ridden loved one at home can take a heavy toll on both the caregiver and the rest of the family. Plans should be made early on to provide relief for the primary caregiver. Hospice recruits and trains volunteers to run errands or attend to nonprofessional chores. Doctors, nurses, and other critical staff persons are on call twenty-four hours a day, seven days a week.

My Grandfather Yellis was the sole caregiver for my grand-mother until she died. He fed her, bathed her, dressed her, and laundered her clothing and bed clothes with little help from Aunt Elsie, who had a paid job. A doctor did visit from time to time and a housekeeper came in to do the cleaning. But if he had had the services of hospice (which did not exist in our area then), his work would have been much easier. I am tempted to say his daily caring for my grandmother shortened his own life, but since he lived to be ninety-five, that is stretching things, is it not? In fact, that need to give his care to his wife may have lengthened his life. He was necessary.

More information about hospice care can be obtained from either of the following organizations:

The National Hospice Organization
1901 North Moore Street, Suite 901
Arlington, VA 22209
(800) 658-8898
www.nho.org

The Hospice Association of America
228 7th Street SE
Washington, DC 20003
(202) 546-4759
www.hospice-america.org

Should the above phone numbers change, call (800) MEDICARE.

Euthanasia and Suicide

Sometimes called "mercy killing," euthanasia is defined as the act of painlessly putting to death a person suffering from an incurable disease or condition. Dr. Joseph Vincent distin-guishes between active and passive euthanasia. The active form is giving patients something that will cause them to die.

Doctor Vincent calls this doctor-assisted suicide, and he opposes it. Passive euthanasia is the discontinuing of all medical treatments and procedures aimed at curing the disease, but taking care of the patient's normal needs for food, water, and air. In addition, patients receive the medications necessary to control pain.

Here is where one's advance medical directive comes into play. If a person specifies that he or she does not want to be kept on a ventilator, then the breathing assistance is also withdrawn. How one understands the matter of suicide is often based in religious teachings and religious values. Personally, we think it is wrong; but who are we to presume how God will judge a person who is so miserable as to take his or her own life? We are confident that a loving God will forgive such a person, and mercifully accept him or her.

We have wondered, for example, if the death of Judith's mother was a death by suicide. She was eighty-six years old and, despite medication and sheer willpower, was barely surviving congestive heart failure. She knew she would soon have to leave her beloved farm for a winter of loneliness, and she chose to stop taking her medications. Some would consider this a suicidal act, as did, apparently, the emergency-room doctor who cruelly chided Judith for allowing such a thing to happen. But we have come to see her choice in a larger context. After the shock and sadness had worn off a bit, we realized that Judith's mother was telling us, her cherished family, that she was still in control of her life—and death.

Saying Good-bye

In Genesis 49 we read the account of Jacob's last words to his twelve sons as he lay dying. He gave each one a special blessing in the form of a prophecy. For Joseph, he saved the finest of the blessings:

"The blessings of your father
   are stronger than the blessings of the eternal mountains,
   the bounties of the everlasting hills;
may they be on the head of Joseph,
   on the brow of him who was set apart from his brothers."
(Gen. 49:26)

After their father's death, Joseph's brothers, fearful of the revenge he would take on them for trying to kill him, asked for his forgiveness. Joseph cried, and so did his brothers. Joseph responded saying, "So have no fear; I myself will provide for you and your little ones" (Gen. 50:21).

Our Luther Crest chaplain, mindful that many families harbor long-standing anger and resentment, says that the death of a parent is an ideal opportunity for forgiveness and kindness. But death arrives via various routes, and families do not always have the opportunity, prior to a loved one's death, for reconciliation or proper good-byes.

A good friend of mine from our Bethlehem Steel days was working with me on our Interfaith Coalition on Poverty not too long ago. He was a strong and healthy man. One morning he awoke with a severe headache. He quickly lost consciousness and in less than a week he was dead. At his viewing, his three sons, who lived in distant parts of the country, were deeply distraught because they had not had the chance to say good-bye to their beloved father. This is a common aspect of grief when a loved one dies suddenly.

On the other hand, hospice care can provide the opportunity for the dying person to say good-bye. Our friend Joan, who lived in Boston, spent several years fighting cervical cancer. She gradually was worn down by the chemotherapy and radiation treatments, and showed no signs of improvement. Finally, the day came when her doctor recommended she begin hospice care in her home. Joan was a strong woman and faced the reality of her oncoming death in a very open manner.

She invited her husband, her children, and all her good friends to pay her individual visits for the purpose of saying good-bye. The visits were harder on the visitors than they were on Joan. But they were frank visits. No one pretended that Joan would recover; instead, they shared memories and expressed their love for one another. At Joan's funeral, I talked with some of her friends who spoke of the extraordinary experience of saying good-bye to a dear friend. Yes, there were tears, but each person told of the beauty of that unforgettable farewell.

The period of hospice care does not always provide such an opportunity to say good-bye. Depending upon the illness, the patient may be in such a condition that the mere recognition of family and friends is not possible. That, unfortunately, is the way it goes with Alzheimer's disease. The disease progresses and, ultimately, results in death. But the development is slow and by the time death draws near, it may not be possible to communicate with a loved one in any meaningful way.

Some Precious Hours

Knowing that the opportunity to say good-bye to our family members may never occur as it did with Joan in her final days, we have invited our four children to visit us individually for a day or so to spend time solely with Judith and then with me. Our children and their families do not live near us, so our family gatherings are usually large affairs that involve our children's spouses and our grandchildren. These are grand times and we welcome every chance to be with them. But with so many of us milling around, there never seems to be an opportunity to spend several hours solely with one of our children.

These visits by our children are not presented as "saying good-bye" days. But they are presented as times to be together as we have never done since they were little, strictly on a one-to-one basis. Our son was the first to respond to our invitation. He drove five hours to be with us for one overnight stay. In the late afternoon of his first day he and I toured our city, visiting such places as the home in which I was born, the hospital where he was born, and the home in which he lived as a baby before we moved to Detroit. He told me about the times he and his children visited the homes where we lived in Detroit and Devon. We visited the gravesites of his four grandparents and their forebears. He saw the schools I attended as a child. All along the way we had good conversations that I think we both will treasure for a long time. He also spent time alone with Judith. Later, our youngest daughter, Jennifer, also drove five hours with her two young children to spend some time with us. Five hours in a car with two little ones is no piece of cake. But she wanted to do it and I will always treasure the time she and I spent alone together.

Our Final Day

There will come the day for each of us when, ultimately, it is over. It will be the end of our mortal life. But it will not be the end. What the transition from mortal life to immortality will be like, none of us knows. We each have our own hopes and expectations. But of one thing we can be certain: The God who sustained and cared for us all the days of our life will not pull down the shade on us when we die.

Judith's understanding of immortality begins with the often-quoted line from Paul's First Letter to the Corinthians: "For now we see in a mirror dimly, but then we shall see face to face." But rather than a mirror, Judith visualizes a sheer curtain. In life we catch only glimpses of God as God works among us. But at death we move through the curtain to another plane of being—the promised immortality.

The God who watched over me as a child of the depression, as the only child in a broken family, as a very shy child in school, as a frightened youth in combat in Europe, as a grateful husband of dear Judith, as a proud father and grandfather of four delightful children and nine beautiful grandchildren, as a thankful member of a host of good friends—that God has one more surprise for me and for you.

As Paul wrote to the church at Rome, nothing will be able to separate us from the love of God in Christ Jesus, our Lord— "neither death nor life." Of that we can be sure.

notes

Chapter 1

1. "A Graying Wealth of Gray Matter" by Joan Ryan, *San Francisco Chronicle* (September 7, 1999): p. A21.
2. *The Barnhart Dictionary of Etymology*, first edition, edited by Robert K. Barnhart (Bronx, NY: H. W. Wilson, 1988).
3. Quoted in *The Oxford English Dictionary*, second edition, vol. XIII (Oxford: Claredon Press, 1989).
4. Quoted in "What to Call People Who Used to Be Old" by Dudley Clendinen, *New York Times* (July 2, 2000): section WK, p.10.
5. "Working for Fun After Retirement" by Hilary Wasson and Suzy Parker, *USA Today* (October 26, 2000): p. A1.
6. "Getting Older Ain't What It Used to Be" by Douglas J. Besharow and Keith Smith, *Washington Post* (August 1, 1999): p. B3.
7. "What to Call People Who Used to Be Old," Clendinen.

Chapter 2

1. *Bowling Alone: The Collapse and Revival of American Community* by Robert D. Putnam (New York: Simon and Schuster, 2000).
2. See, for example, *New York Times* (May 28, 2000); *Wall Street Journal* (May 25, 2000); *Business Week* (June 26, 2000); *Washington Post*, national weekly edition (June 12, 2000); and *Economist* (December 23, 2000).
3. "Are We Bowling Alone and Does It Matter?" by Mark Chaves, *Christian Century* (July 19–26, 2000): p. 754.
4. *Prime Time: How Baby Boomers Will Revolutionize Retirement and Transform America* by Marc Freedman (San Francisco: Perseus Books, 2000).
5. "A New Force in Volunteerism" by Holly Hall, *Chronicle of Philanthropy* vol. X, no. 4 (November 27, 1997): p. 25.
6. "Volunteer Is a Priority, Older Americans Say" by Grant Williams, *Chronicle of Philanthropy* vol. XI, no. 22 (September 1999): p. 1.
7. "A Big New Wrinkle" by Gene Epstein, *Barron's* (September 1, 1999): p. 29.

8. "Older People Want to Work in Retirement, Survey Finds" by Sara Rimer, *New York Times* (September 2, 1999): p. A18.
9. "A Big New Wrinkle," Epstein, p. 30.
10. Ibid.
11. "Busted Boomers: Here's the Wake-up Call" by Brian O'Reilly, *Fortune* (July 24, 1995): p. 52.
12. Survey conducted by Peter D. Hart Research Associates, published September 1999.
13. "Volunteer Service Awaits Retiring Baby Boomers" by Sonia Csenvcsits, *Morning Call* (March 4, 2001): p. B2.
14. "A New Generation of Student Protesters Arises" by Arthur Levine, *Chronicle of Higher Education* vol. 45, issue 25 (February 26, 1999): p. A52.
15. "The Good Works Perk" by Laura Kosa-Feder, *Time* (January 22, 2001): p. B1.
16. *Bowling Alone,* Putnam, p. 35.
17. Ibid., p. 32.
18. Ibid., p. 31.
19. Ibid., p. 33.
20. *Habits of the Heart: Individualism and Commitment in American Life* by Robert Bellah, et al. (Berkeley, CA: University of California Press, 1985).
21. "George vs. Richard" (no author), *U.S. News and World Report* (December 25, 2000): p. 12.
22. *Bowling Alone,* Putnam, p. 36.

Chapter 3

1. *The Random House Dictionary of the English Language,* second edition (New York: Random House, 1997).
2. *The Monday Connection: On Being an Authentic Christian in a Weekday World* by William E. Diehl (San Francisco: HarperSanFrancisco, 1993).
3. *Aging: The Facts* by Nicolas Coni, et al. (Oxford: Oxford University Press, 1992).

Chapter 4

1. "Couples Coping" by Francine Russo, *Time* (November 2001): p. G1.
2. *Consumer Reports Complete Guide to Health Services for Seniors* by Trudy Lieberman and Consumer Reports editors (New York: Three Rivers Press, 2000).

3. "Moving Next Door" by Ben Brown, *Wall Street Journal* (June 5, 2000): p. 12.
4. Ibid.
5. "Keeping the Faith" by Glenn Ruffenach, *Wall Street Journal* (June 5, 2000): p. 13.
6. "Boomers Move in on the Senior Set" by Daniel Costello, *Wall Street Journal* (December 29, 2000): p. W8.
7. "Where to Move When You're Ready to Kick Back" by Susan E. Kuhn, *Fortune* (July 24, 1995): p. 86.
8. "Reaching Across the Miles" by Toyo A. Biddle, *Wall Street Journal* (June 5, 2000): p. 1.

Chapter 5
1. "Nothing Left to Prove" by Dan Wakefield, *MM Magazine* (formerly *Modern Maturity*) (May/June 2001): p 38.
2. *God and Mammon in America* by Robert Wuthnow (New York: The Free Press, 1991): p. 48.
3. Ibid., p. 181.
4. Ibid., p. 175.
5. "Pious Materialism: How Americans View Faith and Money" by Robert Wuthnow, *Christian Century* (March 3, 1993): p. 241.
6. *After Progress* by Anthony O'Hear (London: Bloomsbury, 2000), as quoted in "So Much Affluence, So Little Happiness" by Damon Linker, *Wall Street Journal* (April 20, 2000): p. A24.
7. Quoted in *Freedom of Simplicity* by Richard J. Foster (New York: Harper & Row, 1981): p. 87.
8. *The Politics of Jesus* by John Howard Yoder (Grand Rapids, MI: Eerdmans Publishing Company, 1972): p. 146.
9. "Job Goes, Worries Come" by Christian Berg, *Morning Call* (May 27, 2001): p. A1.
10. "Consumerism" by Craig M. Gay in *The Complete Book of Everyday Christianity* edited by Robert Banks and R. Paul Stevens (Downers Grove, IL: Intervarsity Press, 1997): p. 222.
11. *Celebration of Discipline: The Path to Spiritual Growth* by Richard J. Foster (New York: Harper & Row, 1978): p. 69.
12. *Freedom of Simplicity* by Richard J. Foster (New York: Harper & Row, 1981): p. 3.
13. *Enough Is Enough* by John V. Taylor (Minneapolis: Augsburg Publishing House, 1975).
14. "Politics 2000" by Glenn Ruffenach, *Wall Street Journal* (September 11, 2000): p. 8.

15. "Power Politics" by Glenn Ruffenach, *Wall Street Journal* (September 11, 2000): Encore Section, p. 8.
16. "More Young People Turn Away from Politics and Concentrate Instead on Community Service" by Elizabeth Crowley, *Wall Street Journal* (June 16, 1999): p. A22.
17. "Older Americans Living Longer, Better" by Paul Recer of the Associated Press, *Morning Call* (August 10, 2000): p. A8.
18. "Retirees Becoming Wealthier, Healthier" by Jon E. Hilsenrath, *Wall Street Journal* (May 23, 2001): p. A2.

Chapter 6
1. *Working* by Studs Terkel (New York: Avon Books, 1972): p. xxix.
2. For more on this topic, see *The Monday Connection*, Diehl.
3. "New Economy Denizens Join Ranks of Bankruptcy Filers" Ruth Simon, *Wall Street Journal* (November 23, 2001): p. C1.
4. U.S. Government Poverty Guidelines, effective February 15, 2000.
5. *Nickel and Dimed: On (Not) Getting By in America* by Barbara Ehrenreich (New York: Metropolitan Books, 2001).
6. "AT&T Job Seekers: Take My Cards, Please" by Charles L. P. Fairweather, *New York Times* (December 24, 2000): Business Section, p. 4.
7. "Raw Deals" by Ellen E. Schultz, *Wall Street Journal* (December 27, 2000): p. A1.
8. "A Big New Wrinkle" by Gene Epstein, *Barron's* (September 1999): p. 29.
9. "The Gray Team" by Clare Ansberry, *Wall Street Journal* (February 5, 2001): p. A1.

Chapter 7
1. "Determined to Ease Human Burden" by Madeleine Mathias, *Morning Call* (July 22, 2001): p. E8.
2. *Bowling Alone*, Putnam, p. 117.
3. *Complete Book of Everyday Christianity*, Banks and Stevens, p. 859.
4. "Third Age Elderly Begin to Give a New Definition to Retirement" by Albert R. Hunt, *Wall Street Journal* (March 11, 1999): p. A9.
5. "McCain Bayh Propose Making Service a Response to Sept. 11" by David Broder, *Morning Call* (October 7, 2001): p. A1.
6. "The Virtuous Vacation?" by Susan Carey, *Wall Street Journal* (July 27, 2000): p. B1.
7. "Getting Together" (no author), *AARP Bulletin* (December 2001): p. 16.

Chapter 8

1. *In Search of Faithfulness: Lessons from the Christian Community* by William E. Diehl (Philadelphia: Fortress Press, 1987): p. 78.
2. "Reasons for Giving All You've Got to Give" by Joseph A. Grundfest, *Wall Street Journal* (January 6, 1995): p. A10.
3. "United Way of Lehigh County Misses Its Goal for First Time" by Nichole Radzeivich, *Morning Call* (November 16, 2001): p. A1.
4. "Charitable Giving Surged Again in '99, By an Estimated 9%" by Karen W. Arenson, *New York Times* (May 25, 2000): p. A2.
5. From the Ministry of Money Newsletter edited by Don McClanen (February 1997).

Chapter 9

1. "Fewer Americans Save for Their Retirement" by Glenn Ruffenach, *Wall Street Journal* (May 10, 2001): p. A2.
2. "Opening Your Nest Egg Without Breaking It" by Ellen Hoffman, *Business Week* (July 30, 2001): p. 92.
3. See, for example, Mike McNamee, *Business Week* (July 31, 2000): p. 131.
4. As reported in Ministry of Money Newsletter, (June 2000).
5. "Big Footprints" by Carlos Tejada and Patrick Barta, *Wall Street Journal* (January 7, 2000): p. A1.
6. Ibid.
7. Ibid.
8. "Make No (Big) Mistakes" by Sharon Epperson, *Time* (July 23, 2001): p. 81.
9. "Fewer Americans Save for Their Retirement," Ruffenach.
10. "Pension 101: Companies Find Host of Subtle Ways to Pare Retirement Payouts" by Ellen E. Schultz, *Wall Street Journal* (July 27, 2000): p. A1.
11. Ibid.
12. "Pension Revolt Catches Fire" by Trish Nicholson, *AARP Bulletin* (September 2000): p. 14.
13. "Cut in Health Benefits Squeeze Retirees' Nest Eggs" by Milt Freudenheim, *New York Times* (December 31, 2000): Business Section, p. 8.
14. "Cracks in the Nest Egg: A Look at the Biggest Mistakes Investors are Making with Their Retirement Savings" by Glenn Ruffenach, *Wall Street Journal* (October 22, 2001): Encore Section, p. R6.
15. "Working Full Time Is No Longer Enough" by Jacob M. Schlesinger, *Wall Street Journal* (June 29, 2000): p. A2.

16. "Out of Sight, Out of Mind" (no author), *Economist* (May 2, 2000): p. 27.

Chapter 10
1. "Who Wants to Live Forever?" (no author), *Economist* (December 23, 2000): pp. 23–24.
2. *Good Grief* by Granger Westberg (Philadelphia: Fortress Press, 1961).
3. *To Touch a Grieving Heart: Healing Ways to Help Ourselves and Others Walk the Journey of Grief* video hosted by Kathleen Braza (Salt Lake City. Panacom Incorporated, 1995).
4. *Good Grief,* Westberg, p. 34.
5. "Giving More Patients a Good Death" by Mary C. Hickley, *Business Week* (November 20, 2000): p. 166.
6. *Dying Well: Peace and Possibilities at the End of Life* edited by Dr. Ira Byock (New York: Riverhead Books, 1997): p. 215.
7. "A Kinder, Gentler Death" by John Cloud, *Time* (September 18, 2002): p. 67.
8. *How We Die* by Sherwin P. Nuland (New York: Knopf, 1994): p. 265.

OTHER RESOURCES FROM AUGSBURG

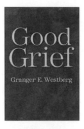

Good Grief by Granger E. Westberg
64 pages, 0-8006-1114-4
Since its first edition in 1962, *Good Grief* has become
a standard resource for people grieving losses. With
gentle wisdom and acute insight, Westberg guides
the reader through the stages of grief.

How to Keep a Spiritual Journal
by Ron Klug
144 pages, 0-8066-4357-9
An indispensable guide that shows new ways to care
for your soul with prayer, spiritual readings, and
journal exercises. This book will help you understand
your spiritual journey.

A Prayerbook for Spiritual Friends
by Madeleine L'Engle and Luci Shaw
96 pages, 0-8066-3892-3
A collection of read-aloud prayers for friends.
This book will draw friends closer, to God and
to each other.

Prayers for the Later Years
by Malcolm Boyd
128 pages, 0-8066-4194-0

A collection of real-life prayers for everyone who is growing
older. Malcolm Boyd addresses the struggles and blessings of
life's later years in this wonderful collection of brief prayers.

Available wherever books are sold.